La Palma

Travel Guide 2025

Trails, Traditions, and Timeless Beauty

Gregory N. Hickman

Copyright © **Gregory N. Hickman, 2024.**

All rights reserved. No part of this publication may be reproduced, distributed, or transmitted in any form or by any means, including photocopying, recording, or other electronic or mechanical methods, without the prior written permission of the publisher, except in the case of brief quotations embodied in critical reviews and certain other non-commercial uses permitted by copyright law.

Contents

My La Palma Trip — 1

Introduction — 6
Historical Background — *6*
Cultural Highlights — *10*

Planning Your Trip — 15
Best time to travel — *15*
Transportation options — *19*
Visa Requirements — *22*

Accommodation Options — 28
Luxury Hotels and Resorts — *28*
Budget-Friendly Stays — *31*
Unique Lodging Experiences — *33*

Exploring Santa Cruz de La Palma — 39
Historical Landmarks — *39*
Museums and Galleries — *43*

Natural Wonders and Outdoor Activities — 48
La Caldera de Taburiente National Park — *48*
Volcano Hiking Trails — *52*
Beaches and Natural Pools — *56*

Stargazing and Astronomical Tourism	*60*
Coastal Adventures	**65**
Watersports and Diving	*65*
Coastal Villages to Visit	*70*
Boat Tours and Excursions	*75*
Culinary Delights	**81**
Traditional Canarian Cuisine	*81*
Must-Try Dishes and Restaurants	*84*
Local Markets and Food Festivals	*90*
Wine and Craft Beer Tasting	*94*
Cultural and Art Experiences	**98**
Local Art and Craftsmanship	*98*
Music and Dance Traditions	*103*
Useful Tips	**108**
Money Matters	*108*
Useful Contacts and emergency Information	*111*
7 Days Itinerary	**115**
Estimated Budget for 7 Days	**123**

My La Palma Trip

My adventure began in Santa Cruz de La Palma, the island's vibrant capital. The town's charming blend of history and modernity was immediately apparent as I wandered through its cobblestone streets, lined with colorful colonial-style houses and adorned with intricate wooden balconies. I marveled at the well-preserved architecture, a testament to the island's rich past, and visited iconic landmarks such as Plaza España, the heart of the city, and the Iglesia de El Salvador, a magnificent church that showcases a blend of architectural styles.

Los Tilos Forest
Eager to explore La Palma's natural beauty, I ventured north to Los Tilos Forest, a UNESCO Biosphere Reserve that promised an immersive experience in nature. The scenic drive through winding roads offered glimpses of the island's diverse landscapes, from rugged coastlines to lush greenery and volcanic peaks.

Upon reaching Los Tilos, I embarked on a hike through the verdant laurel forest, where the air was filled with the scent of damp earth and the sounds of chirping birds. The trail led me deeper into the forest, revealing hidden waterfalls and streams, creating a sense of tranquility and wonder. The highlight of the hike was a cascading waterfall, where I paused to appreciate the serene beauty of the surroundings and the power of nature's artistry.

San Andrés y Sauces
My journey continued to the charming town of San Andrés y Sauces, where I explored its historic center, with its traditional Canarian architecture and picturesque plazas. The Church of San Andrés, a beautiful example of the island's religious heritage, and the Plaza de Montserrat, a charming square surrounded by

colorful houses and cafes, offered a glimpse into the town's unique character.

In the afternoon, I discovered the natural wonder of Charco Azul, a series of seawater pools formed by volcanic rock. The crystal-clear water, sheltered from the waves of the Atlantic, provided a refreshing escape from the midday sun. I spent the afternoon swimming in the pools, sunbathing on the surrounding rocks, and enjoying the stunning coastal views.

Caldera de Taburiente National Park
One of the highlights of my La Palma adventure was a visit to the Caldera de Taburiente National Park, a geological wonder and a haven for nature lovers. Starting at the Visitor Center in El Paso, I gathered maps and information before setting off on a hike through the park's diverse landscapes.

The park's well-marked trails led me through a fascinating array of volcanic formations, from craters and cones to lava flows and unique rock formations. I hiked through lush forests, crossed flowing streams, and marveled at the dramatic scenery that unfolded before me. The challenging ascent to the Roque de Los Muchachos, the highest point on the island, was rewarded with breathtaking panoramic views that stretched across the entire island and out to the vast expanse of the Atlantic Ocean.

I enjoyed a picnic lunch amidst the stunning scenery, surrounded by the park's unique flora and fauna. The Caldera de Taburiente is a biodiversity hotspot, home to a variety of endemic plant and animal species that have adapted to the island's volcanic environment.

In the evening, I visited the Museum of the Silk Road in El Paso, where I learned about La Palma's fascinating silk-making tradition and its historical connections to the Silk Road trade routes. The museum's exhibits showcased the intricate process of silk production, from silkworm cultivation to the weaving of exquisite textiles.

Tazacorte and Puerto Naos: Exploring the West Coast

My exploration of La Palma continued on the west coast, where I visited the charming town of Tazacorte, known for its sunny climate, historic architecture, and banana plantations. I delved into the island's agricultural heritage at the Banana Museum, learning about the history and cultivation of bananas, one of La Palma's main exports.

After a delicious seafood lunch at a beachfront restaurant in Tazacorte, I headed to Puerto Naos, a popular beach destination renowned for its black sand beach and vibrant atmosphere. The beach, framed by palm trees and the sparkling Atlantic Ocean, was a perfect spot for relaxation and recreation. I spent the afternoon swimming in the clear waters, sunbathing on the black sand, and trying out some water sports, such as snorkeling, to explore the underwater world.

Fuencaliente

My journey took me to the southern tip of La Palma, where I explored the unique volcanic landscapes of Fuencaliente. I started my day at the San Antonio Volcano Visitor Center, learning about the island's volcanic history and the fascinating geological processes that have shaped its terrain.

The hike around the San Antonio and Teneguía volcanoes was a captivating experience, with stark volcanic landscapes, lava flows, and panoramic views of the Atlantic Ocean. In the afternoon, I visited the Salinas de Fuencaliente, where sea salt is harvested using traditional methods, creating a mesmerizing landscape of white salt crystals against the black volcanic soil.

I enjoyed a delicious lunch at a nearby restaurant, where the dishes featured locally harvested salt, adding a unique flavor to the cuisine. The day concluded with a visit to a local winery, where I sampled La Palma's renowned Malvasia wines, known for their distinctive character and volcanic influence.

Puntallana and Los Sauces
Continuing my exploration of La Palma, I headed to the east coast to visit the charming towns of Puntallana and Los Sauces. In Puntallana, I visited the Church of San Juan Bautista, a beautiful example of Canarian religious architecture, and the Casa Luján, a traditional Canarian house turned museum, showcasing local crafts, customs, and traditions.

In Los Sauces, I strolled through the historic center, admiring the traditional architecture and visiting the Church of Nuestra Señora de Montserrat and the main square, a hub of local life and activity. The afternoon was spent exploring the lush trails of Los Tilos Forest, a UNESCO Biosphere Reserve that protects a unique ecosystem of laurel forests and waterfalls.

Barlovento
My journey concluded with a visit to Barlovento, a picturesque village known for its iconic dragon tree, a symbol of the Canary Islands. I explored the town's charming streets, admired the traditional architecture, and enjoyed the serene atmosphere. The dragon tree, with its unique shape and ancient history, is a testament to the island's natural heritage and cultural significance.

Farewell to La Palma
As my La Palma adventure came to an end, I spent my last day relaxing on one of the island's beautiful beaches, soaking up the sun and reflecting on the incredible experiences I had enjoyed. I savored a farewell lunch at a beachfront restaurant, enjoying the fresh seafood and local specialties one last time.

In the afternoon, I explored the shops and markets of Santa Cruz de La Palma, searching for souvenirs to take home as reminders of my trip. I found handmade pottery, embroidered textiles, and La Palma's famous cigars, each representing the island's unique craftsmanship and cultural heritage.

As I departed from La Palma, I carried with me a treasure trove of memories, photographs, and souvenirs that would forever remind me of this enchanting island. The warmth of the sun, the vibrant colors of the landscapes, the friendly smiles of the locals, and the thrill of exploring new horizons would stay with me long after I returned home. La Palma, with its unique blend of adventure, relaxation, and cultural immersion, had truly captured my heart.

Introduction
Historical Background

The Benahoaritas

Long before European ships reached its shores, La Palma was home to the Benahoaritas, an indigenous Guanche people who arrived on the island around the 3rd century BC. These early settlers, believed to have Berber origins, established a unique and thriving culture that adapted to the island's volcanic landscapes and fertile valleys.

The Benahoaritas were skilled farmers, cultivating crops such as barley, wheat, and legumes. They also practiced herding, raising goats and sheep, and were adept at fishing, utilizing the resources of the surrounding ocean. Their culture was deeply intertwined with the island's natural environment, with sacred sites scattered across the landscape, where they worshipped a pantheon of gods.

The Benahoaritas lived in cave dwellings, taking advantage of the island's volcanic formations, and practiced mummification, preserving the bodies of their deceased in a testament to their beliefs in an afterlife. Their unique language, customs, and social structures reflected their isolation and adaptation to the island's environment.

The Arrival of the Conquistadors

The early 15th century marked a turning point in La Palma's history with the arrival of European explorers. The island, strategically located in the Atlantic Ocean, caught the attention of Spanish conquistadors seeking to expand the Spanish Empire. In 1493, Alonso Fernández de Lugo led a Spanish expedition to La Palma, aiming to conquer the island and claim its resources.

The Benahoaritas fiercely resisted the Spanish conquest, engaging in several battles to defend their homeland. However, the superior weaponry and tactics of the Spanish eventually led to their subjugation. The conquest was completed in 1493, marking the beginning of Spanish rule and the integration of La Palma into the growing Spanish Empire.

Colonial Transformation
The Spanish colonization of La Palma ushered in an era of significant transformation. The Spanish introduced new agricultural practices, including the cultivation of sugar cane, which became a major economic driver for the island. La Palma's fertile volcanic soil and favorable climate proved ideal for sugar production, attracting settlers and laborers from across the Spanish Empire and beyond.

The island's strategic location in the Atlantic Ocean also made it a crucial stopover point for ships traveling between Europe, Africa, and the Americas. Santa Cruz de La Palma, the island's capital, flourished as a bustling port city, becoming a hub for trade and commerce. Merchants exchanged goods such as sugar, wine, and tobacco, bringing wealth and prosperity to the island.

This economic boom led to the construction of grand homes, churches, and public buildings, many of which still stand today as architectural reminders of La Palma's colonial past. The island's prosperity attracted wealthy merchants and nobility, who established a social hierarchy and influenced the island's cultural development.

Challenges and Resilience
The wealth generated from trade and agriculture also attracted unwanted attention. In the late 16th century, La Palma faced the threat of pirate attacks, with renowned privateers like Francis Drake targeting the island's riches. The residents of La Palma

responded by constructing fortifications and lookout towers to protect against these raids, some of which can still be seen along the island's coastline, serving as reminders of the challenges faced during this era.

The 18th century brought economic shifts as the sugar industry declined due to competition from other regions. However, La Palma's resilience and adaptability led to the diversification of its economy. The cultivation of wine, tobacco, and silk gained prominence, with La Palma's vineyards producing a sweet wine known as "Malvasia" that gained international acclaim. The island's silk industry also flourished, with La Palma becoming renowned for its high-quality silk products.

Navigating Modernity
In the 19th century, La Palma faced further economic challenges due to the decline of traditional industries and competition from other regions. However, the island's ability to adapt led to the introduction of banana cultivation in the late 19th century, revitalizing the agricultural sector. Bananas remain a significant export product for La Palma today, contributing to the island's economic stability.

The 20th century brought new challenges and opportunities as La Palma navigated the complexities of modernity. The island's strategic location continued to play a role during World War II, and post-war recovery efforts focused on improving infrastructure and diversifying the economy. Tourism emerged as a key industry, capitalizing on La Palma's natural beauty, mild climate, and unique cultural heritage.

In recent decades, La Palma has positioned itself as a leader in astronomical research. The island's clear skies and low levels of light pollution make it an ideal location for observatories. The Roque de los Muchachos Observatory, situated at one of the highest points on the island, houses some of the world's most advanced telescopes, attracting scientists and researchers from around the globe. This focus on astronomy has not only contributed to scientific knowledge but also spurred a new wave of tourism, with visitors drawn to the island's stargazing opportunities and astronomical facilities.

Preserving Cultural Heritage
Throughout its history, La Palma has maintained a strong sense of cultural identity. Festivals, music, dance, and traditional crafts continue to play an integral role in the island's social fabric, connecting the present generation with its rich past. Events such as the Bajada de la Virgen de las Nieves, a quadrennial celebration that involves bringing a statue of the Virgin Mary from its mountain sanctuary to the capital, showcase La Palma's unique cultural heritage and draw visitors from around the world.

La Palma Today
Today, La Palma stands as a testament to the resilience and adaptability of its people. The island's historical journey from indigenous settlement to a modern hub of science and tourism reflects its ability to embrace change while preserving its unique cultural legacy. As La Palma looks to the future, it remains committed to sustainable development, ensuring that its natural beauty, cultural heritage, and pristine environment are protected for generations to come.

Cultural Highlights
Festivals and Celebrations

La Palma's calendar is punctuated by a vibrant array of festivals and celebrations that showcase the island's deep-rooted traditions, religious devotion, and community spirit.

Bajada de la Virgen de las Nieves: This quadrennial event, held in the capital city of Santa Cruz de La Palma, is a grand celebration in honor of the island's patron saint, Our Lady of the Snows. The festival is a highlight of La Palma's cultural calendar, drawing participants and spectators from across the island and beyond. The festivities include processions, where the statue of the Virgin is carried through the streets amidst a sea of devotees, traditional dances that have been passed down through generations, concerts featuring local and international musicians, and a range of cultural activities that showcase the island's heritage. The pinnacle of the event is the "Bajada," a solemn and elaborate ceremony where the statue of the Virgin is brought down from her mountain sanctuary to the city, accompanied by music, dance, and expressions of faith.

Fiesta de Los Indianos: Celebrated during Carnival, the Fiesta de Los Indianos is a unique and exuberant event that commemorates the return of La Palma's emigrants from Latin America, particularly Cuba. Participants dress in all-white attire, reminiscent of the colonial era, and engage in a playful battle of talcum powder, creating a cloud of white that envelops the streets of Santa Cruz de La Palma. The festival is a joyous celebration of the island's connection to its diaspora, with music, dance, and a lively atmosphere that captures the spirit of Carnival.

Traditional Music and Dance

Music and dance are integral to La Palma's cultural identity, expressing the soul of the island and its people. The island boasts a rich tradition of folk music, with the "Isas" and "Folías" being the most popular forms. These traditional songs, often featuring heartfelt lyrics that speak of love, loss, and the beauty of the island, are accompanied by instruments such as the timple (a small, five-stringed guitar unique to the Canary Islands), guitars, and castanets. The rhythms and melodies of La Palma's folk music reflect the island's history, the influence of various cultures, and the emotions of its people.

Folk dance is also an essential part of La Palma's cultural celebrations, with traditional dances performed during festivals and community gatherings. The Danza de los Enanos (Dance of the Dwarfs), performed during the Bajada de la Virgen de las Nieves, is a particularly famous and captivating dance. Participants, dressed in elaborate costumes that transform them into "dwarfs," perform intricate and humorous routines, creating a spectacle that is both entertaining and culturally significant.

Art and Craftsmanship

La Palma's artistic heritage is evident in its traditional crafts and contemporary arts scene, showcasing the creativity and skill of its people. The island is renowned for its fine embroidery and lacework, a tradition passed down through generations of skilled artisans. The delicate designs and meticulous craftsmanship are showcased in various products, from tablecloths and clothing to decorative items that adorn homes and add a touch of elegance to everyday life.

Pottery is another traditional craft with deep roots in La Palma's culture. The "alfarería" of La Palma involves creating beautiful and functional ceramic pieces using traditional methods and designs. These ceramics often feature intricate patterns and natural motifs, reflecting the island's connection to its volcanic landscapes and the surrounding environment.

In the realm of contemporary art, La Palma boasts a thriving arts scene, with numerous galleries and cultural centers showcasing the works of local and international artists. The Cultural Center CajaCanarias in Santa Cruz de La Palma is a hub for artistic expression, hosting exhibitions, performances, and cultural events throughout the year. The island's stunning landscapes and unique light have also attracted many painters and photographers, who find endless inspiration in its natural beauty.

Gastronomy
La Palma's cuisine is a delicious reflection of its cultural heritage and natural abundance. Traditional recipes, passed down through generations, utilize fresh, local ingredients and simple yet flavorful preparations that highlight the island's unique flavors.

A staple of La Palma's gastronomy is "papas arrugadas" (wrinkled potatoes), small potatoes boiled in their skins with a generous amount of sea salt until they become tender and wrinkled. They are typically served with "mojo" sauce, a tangy and flavorful condiment made from garlic, olive oil, and local spices. Mojo comes in two main varieties: Mojo Rojo (red sauce), made with red peppers, and Mojo Verde (green sauce), made with green peppers or cilantro.

Seafood plays a prominent role in La Palma's cuisine, given its island location and access to fresh catches from the Atlantic Ocean. Fresh fish, octopus, and prawns are commonly featured in dishes, often grilled or cooked in stews that showcase the island's culinary traditions. "Sancocho," a traditional fish stew made with salted fish, potatoes, and a variety of vegetables, is a must-try dish that exemplifies the island's connection to the sea.

The island's fertile volcanic soil also supports the cultivation of a variety of fruits and vegetables, including bananas, avocados, and sweet potatoes. These ingredients find their way into numerous dishes, adding freshness and vibrancy to the local cuisine.

La Palma is also known for its wines, produced from grapes grown in the island's unique volcanic soil. The Malvasia grape, in particular, is renowned for producing sweet wines with a distinct flavor profile that reflects the island's terroir. Visitors can explore local vineyards and wineries, enjoying tours and tastings that offer insight into the island's winemaking traditions and the unique characteristics of its wines.

Architecture and Historic Sites
La Palma's architectural heritage is a testament to its rich history and cultural influences, with well-preserved buildings and charming towns that transport visitors back in time.

The capital, Santa Cruz de La Palma, is a treasure trove of colonial architecture, with beautifully preserved buildings lining its cobblestone streets. The historic center is home to numerous landmarks, including the Church of El Salvador, a stunning example of Renaissance and Baroque architecture. The church's intricate woodwork and beautiful altarpieces are a testament to the craftsmanship of the period.

Another architectural gem is the Real Castillo de Santa Catalina, a 17th-century fortress built to protect the city from pirate attacks. The well-preserved structure offers a glimpse into the island's defensive history and provides panoramic views of the coast.

In San Andrés y Sauces, visitors can explore the Church of San Andrés Apostol, one of the oldest churches on the island, with its Mudejar-style wooden ceiling and beautifully carved altars. The nearby Los Tilos Forest, a UNESCO Biosphere Reserve, adds to the charm of this region, offering lush, verdant landscapes for nature lovers.

Natural Heritage and Conservation
La Palma's cultural identity is deeply intertwined with its natural heritage. The island is a UNESCO Biosphere Reserve, recognized for its diverse ecosystems and commitment to conservation. The Caldera de Taburiente National Park is a prime example of this dedication, with its dramatic landscapes, including deep ravines, waterfalls, and dense forests, providing a sanctuary for a variety of flora and fauna.

Stargazing is another unique aspect of La Palma's cultural and natural heritage. The island's clear skies and minimal light pollution have made it one of the world's premier locations for astronomical observation. The Roque de los Muchachos Observatory, perched atop the island's highest peak, is home to some of the most advanced telescopes in the world, contributing to scientific discoveries and attracting astrotourism enthusiasts.

Literary and Intellectual Contributions
La Palma has also made significant contributions to literature and intellectual thought. The island has been home to numerous poets, writers, and thinkers whose works reflect the island's beauty, history, and cultural depth. José Pérez Vidal, a prominent historian and ethnographer, dedicated his life to documenting the traditions and folklore of the Canary Islands, preserving valuable aspects of La Palma's cultural heritage for future generations.

The island's literary scene is celebrated through various events and festivals, such as the "Semana del Libro" (Book Week) in Santa Cruz de La Palma, which features readings, workshops, and discussions with authors, fostering a love of literature and intellectual exchange.

Planning Your Trip
Best time to travel

Spring
Spring in La Palma is a time of rebirth and rejuvenation. The island awakens from its mild winter with a burst of colorful blooms, lush greenery, and a vibrant energy that permeates the air. Temperatures during this season are typically pleasant, ranging from 18°C to 24°C (64°F to 75°F), making it ideal for outdoor activities and exploration.

> **Nature at its Best:** Spring is the perfect time to immerse yourself in La Palma's natural beauty. The island's network of hiking trails comes alive with the sights and sounds of nature. The famous trails in the Caldera de Taburiente National Park, a geological wonder with its deep caldera and volcanic peaks, are particularly stunning in spring, with waterfalls cascading down the cliffs and wildflowers blanketing the meadows. The Ruta de los Volcanes trail offers a challenging but rewarding hike through volcanic terrain, showcasing the island's dramatic geological formations.
>
> **Birdwatching Paradise:** For bird enthusiasts, spring is a prime time to observe La Palma's diverse avian population. The island's varied habitats, from lush forests to rugged cliffs and coastal areas, attract a wide range of bird species, including migratory birds that make their way to La Palma during this season.
>
> **Cultural Celebrations:** Spring is also a time for cultural celebrations in La Palma. Semana Santa (Holy Week) is a significant religious event observed with solemn

processions, traditional ceremonies, and vibrant displays of faith in towns and villages across the island.

Summer

Summer in La Palma is a time for beach days, warm sunshine, and vibrant festivities. The island's temperatures rise to a comfortable range of 20°C to 28°C (68°F to 82°F), making it ideal for enjoying the coastal beauty and engaging in water activities.

Beach Bliss: La Palma's beaches beckon in the summer, offering a variety of options for relaxation and recreation. Popular spots like Puerto Naos and Playa de Nogales attract visitors with their black volcanic sand, clear waters, and stunning coastal scenery. Water activities such as swimming, snorkeling, and diving are at their best during this time, with excellent visibility and warm sea temperatures.

Stargazing Paradise: La Palma is renowned for its clear skies and minimal light pollution, making it one of the best places in the world for stargazing. The summer months offer exceptional opportunities for astronomy enthusiasts to marvel at the celestial wonders. The island's Roque de los Muchachos Observatory, home to some of the world's most advanced telescopes, provides guided tours and night sky observations, allowing visitors to explore the universe and learn about astronomical research.

Festivals and Fun: Summer is also a time for vibrant festivals and cultural celebrations in La Palma. The Fiesta de la Patrona de Los Llanos de Aridane in August is a highlight, with music, dance, traditional Canarian costumes, and a spectacular firework display that illuminates the night sky.

Autumn

Autumn in La Palma is a season of mellow warmth, fewer crowds, and a captivating display of natural beauty. The temperatures remain comfortable, ranging from 19°C to 25°C (66°F to 77°F), making it ideal for both outdoor adventures and relaxing escapes.

> **Harvest Bounty:** Autumn is harvest time on the island, and visitors can experience the abundance of fresh produce and local flavors. Vineyards come alive with the activity of grape harvesting, and wine enthusiasts can indulge in wine-tasting tours, savoring the unique character of La Palma's wines, influenced by the island's volcanic soil.
>
> **Hiking and Exploration:** The pleasant autumn weather makes it an excellent time for hiking and exploring La Palma's diverse terrains. The island's trails are less crowded during this season, offering a more tranquil and immersive experience in nature. The Los Tilos Forest, a UNESCO Biosphere Reserve, is particularly enchanting in autumn, with its lush greenery and serene ambiance.
>
> **Cultural Events:** Autumn also hosts cultural events that celebrate the island's traditions and heritage. The Fiesta de la Vendimia in Fuencaliente celebrates the grape harvest with parades, music, and wine tastings, while the Virgen de la Luz festival in September features religious processions and local customs.

Winter

Winter in La Palma is mild and pleasant, with temperatures ranging from 15°C to 21°C (59°F to 70°F). The island's subtropical climate ensures that even during the winter months, it remains a welcoming destination for outdoor activities and relaxation.

Astronomical Observation: Winter skies in La Palma are exceptionally clear, making it another excellent season for stargazing. The Roque de los Muchachos Observatory offers winter programs that highlight the best celestial events, including meteor showers and planetary alignments, providing a unique opportunity to witness the wonders of the universe.

Outdoor Activities: While the higher altitudes might experience a bit of a chill, the coastal areas remain warm enough for leisurely strolls along the beaches and enjoying water activities. The island's natural pools, such as Charco Azul, offer a unique swimming experience with their crystal-clear waters and volcanic formations.

Festive Celebrations: The winter season brings festive cheer to La Palma, with Christmas and New Year celebrated with traditional decorations, nativity scenes, and local delicacies. The Three Kings Parade in January is a highlight, with vibrant processions and celebrations throughout the island.

Cultural Exploration: Winter is also an ideal time to delve into La Palma's cultural heritage. Visiting the island's museums and historical sites is a comfortable endeavor with the mild weather. The Museum of the Island of La Palma in Santa Cruz offers fascinating insights into the island's history, culture, and traditions.

Transportation options
From Europe
Europeans have several convenient options for reaching La Palma, making it an accessible getaway for those seeking a unique island experience.

>**By Air:** La Palma is well-connected to various European cities through a network of direct flights. Airlines such as TUI, British Airways, and Transavia offer direct flights from major hubs like London, Amsterdam, and Düsseldorf, making it easy for travelers from these cities to reach the island quickly and comfortably. Condor also operates direct flights from several German cities, including Düsseldorf, Munich, and Berlin, providing further options for German travelers.

For those departing from other European cities, connecting flights are readily available. Major airports in Spain, such as Madrid and Barcelona, serve as convenient hubs for connecting flights to La Palma. Additionally, travelers can connect through other Canary Islands, such as Tenerife and Gran Canaria, offering the opportunity to explore multiple islands during their trip.

>**By Ferry:** While less common than air travel, reaching La Palma by ferry is a viable option for those who prefer a scenic sea journey. Ferries operate from ports in mainland Spain, such as Cádiz and Huelva, offering a leisurely way to travel to the island while enjoying the vastness of the Atlantic Ocean. The ferry trip typically takes around 24 to 30 hours, depending on the route and weather conditions, providing ample time to relax, unwind, and anticipate the beauty of La Palma.

From North America

Traveling to La Palma from North America typically involves a connecting flight through a major European hub.

> **By Air:** Direct flights from North America to La Palma are limited, but travelers can easily connect through major European airports that offer direct flights to the island. London, Amsterdam, and Düsseldorf are popular hubs for connecting flights, providing convenient options for travelers from various North American cities. The total travel time can vary depending on the chosen route and layovers, but it generally takes around 12 to 15 hours to reach La Palma from North America.
>
> **By Cruise:** For those seeking a more leisurely and luxurious travel experience, some cruise lines include La Palma as a port of call on their itineraries. Travelers can embark on a cruise from various departure points in North America and enjoy a stopover in La Palma as part of their journey. This option provides a unique way to experience the island, combining the relaxation and amenities of a cruise ship with the opportunity to explore La Palma's natural beauty and cultural attractions.

From South America

Similar to travelers from North America, those departing from South America typically need to connect through a European hub to reach La Palma.

> **By Air:** Direct flights from South America to La Palma are limited, but travelers can connect through major European airports such as Madrid, Barcelona, or London. Airlines like Iberia, British Airways, and TUI offer connecting flights that can transport travelers to La Palma, providing a convenient, albeit longer, journey.

> **By Cruise:** Cruise lines also offer an alternative way to reach La Palma from South America. Some cruise itineraries include La Palma as a port of call, allowing travelers to enjoy a stopover on the island as part of their cruise vacation. This option provides a unique perspective of La Palma, combining the relaxation and amenities of a cruise ship with the opportunity to explore the island's natural wonders and cultural heritage.

From Africa

Travelers from Africa can reach La Palma through similar options to those from North and South America.

> **By Air:** Direct flights from African cities to La Palma are limited, but travelers can connect through major European hubs such as Madrid, Barcelona, or London. Airlines like Iberia, British Airways, and TUI offer connecting flights that can take travelers to La Palma, providing a convenient way to reach the island.

> **By Cruise:** Some cruise lines include La Palma as a port of call on their itineraries, offering travelers from Africa the opportunity to enjoy a stopover on the island as part of their cruise vacation.

From Asia and Oceania

Travelers from Asia and Oceania typically need to connect through a European hub to reach La Palma.

> **By Air:** Direct flights from Asia and Oceania to La Palma are limited, but travelers can connect through major European airports such as London, Amsterdam, and Düsseldorf, which offer direct flights to the island. The total travel time can vary depending on the chosen route

and layovers, but it generally takes around 12 to 15 hours to reach La Palma from these regions.

By Cruise: Some cruise lines include La Palma as a port of call on their itineraries, offering travelers from Asia and Oceania a unique way to experience the island as part of a larger cruise vacation.

Visa Requirements
For EU, EFTA, and Schengen Area Citizens
Citizens of the European Union (EU), as well as Iceland, Liechtenstein, Norway (EFTA countries), and Switzerland (part of the Schengen Area), enjoy the privilege of visa-free travel to La Palma. They can enter the island with their national identity document or a valid passport, without any additional visa requirements. This freedom of movement allows them to stay in La Palma for up to 90 days within a 180-day period, providing ample time to explore the island's beauty and experience its unique charm.

For Non-EU, EFTA, and Schengen Area Citizens
Travelers from countries outside the EU, EFTA, and Schengen Area generally require a visa to enter La Palma. However, there are exceptions and specific regulations depending on your nationality and the purpose of your visit.

Short-Stay Visas: Nationals from many countries, including the United States, Canada, Australia, New Zealand, Japan, and Israel, benefit from visa-free travel for short stays in La Palma. These travelers can enter the island without a visa for up to 90 days within a 180-day period, allowing for ample time to explore the island's attractions and experience its culture. However, it's crucial to ensure that your passport is valid for at least three months beyond your planned departure from Spain and that it was issued within the last 10 years.

Visa Exemptions: Some countries have specific visa exemption agreements with Spain, allowing their citizens to visit La Palma without a visa for short stays. It's always advisable to check with the Spanish embassy or consulate in your country to obtain the most up-to-date information on visa requirements and exemptions for your nationality.

Long-Stay Visas: If you plan to stay in La Palma for more than 90 days, you will need to apply for a long-stay visa. This applies to any foreigner who wishes to reside in Spain for an extended period, regardless of the purpose of their stay, with the exception of EU, EFTA, and Schengen Area citizens. Long-stay visas can be granted for various purposes, including work, study, family reunification, or retirement. The application process and requirements for long-stay visas vary depending on the purpose of your stay and your nationality. It's essential to contact the Spanish embassy or consulate in your country well in advance of your planned trip to gather the necessary information and initiate the visa application process.

International Teleworkers (Digital Nomads): Spain has introduced a visa specifically for international teleworkers, also known as digital nomads. This visa allows non-EU citizens to reside in Spain, including La Palma, for up to one year while working remotely for companies located outside of Spain. This visa is ideal for individuals who wish to experience the island life while maintaining their remote work commitments. The digital nomad visa has specific requirements and application procedures, so it's essential to research the details and ensure you meet the eligibility criteria before applying.

Airport Transit Visa: Certain nationalities require an airport transit visa even if they are only transiting through a Spanish airport, including those in La Palma. It's crucial to check whether this applies to your nationality and, if necessary, apply for the transit visa before your trip. Failing to obtain a required transit visa can result in denied boarding or delays in your travel plans.

Additional Requirements

Regardless of your visa status, all travelers must meet certain entry requirements to ensure a smooth arrival in La Palma.

Passport Validity: Your passport must be valid for at least three months beyond your planned departure from Spain. Additionally, the passport must have been issued within the last 10 years. It's crucial to check your passport's validity well in advance of your trip to avoid any issues at the border.

Proof of Financial Means: Immigration authorities may ask travelers to provide proof of sufficient financial means to support themselves during their stay in La Palma. This can include cash, traveler's cheques, bank statements, credit card statements, or a letter of financial support from a sponsor. The required amount may vary, but it's generally recommended to have access to at least 100 Euros per person per day of your intended stay, with a minimum of 900 Euros or equivalent in foreign currency.

Return or Onward Travel: You may be required to show proof of return or onward travel, such as a return ticket to your home country or a travel itinerary that demonstrates your plans to leave Spain within the permitted timeframe. This requirement is to ensure that you do not intend to overstay your visa or permitted duration of stay.

Accommodation Reservations: Proof of accommodation, such as a hotel booking confirmation, Airbnb reservation, or a letter of invitation from a host, may be required upon entry. This documentation confirms that you have a place to stay during your visit to La Palma.

Packing Tips
Clothing Essentials
La Palma's subtropical climate generally offers pleasant temperatures year-round, but its microclimates and varied landscapes mean you'll need to be prepared for a range of conditions.

Lightweight Clothing: Pack a variety of T-shirts, shorts, and light pants made from breathable fabrics like cotton or linen. These will keep you comfortable during the warmer days, especially when exploring the coast or lower altitudes.

Layers for Cooler Evenings: Evenings, particularly in the higher altitudes or during the winter months, can be cooler. Pack layers such as long-sleeve shirts, light sweaters, and a jacket to adapt to changing temperatures. A fleece jacket or a light down jacket can be particularly useful for added warmth without excessive bulk.

Rain Gear: La Palma's lush, green areas and mountainous regions can experience rainfall, especially during the winter and spring months. A lightweight, waterproof jacket or poncho is essential to keep you dry during unexpected showers. Consider a packable rain jacket that can be easily folded and stored in your daypack when not in use.

Swimwear: La Palma boasts beautiful beaches and natural pools, making swimwear a must-have item. Pack a couple of swimsuits so you can rotate them and always have a dry one ready. Consider a rash guard for added sun protection during water activities.

Hiking Gear: If you plan to explore La Palma's extensive network of hiking trails, appropriate gear is crucial. Comfortable, moisture-wicking clothing will help regulate your body temperature and keep you dry during strenuous hikes. Sturdy hiking boots or shoes with good ankle support and traction are essential for navigating uneven terrain. Don't forget a hat for sun protection and consider hiking socks to prevent blisters and ensure comfort on long walks.

Footwear

Choosing the right footwear is crucial for navigating La Palma's varied terrain and activities.

Comfortable Walking Shoes: Comfortable walking shoes or sneakers are essential for exploring the island's towns, villages, and cities. Look for shoes that offer good support and cushioning for walking on cobblestone streets and uneven surfaces.

Flip-Flops or Sandals: For beach days and casual outings, pack a pair of flip-flops or sandals. They are easy to slip on and off, making them perfect for beach visits and relaxing by the pool.

Water Shoes: If you plan on exploring rocky shores, natural pools, or engaging in water sports, water shoes can protect your feet from sharp rocks and provide better traction on slippery surfaces.

Accessories

Accessories can enhance your comfort and enjoyment during your La Palma adventure.

> **Sun Protection:** The Canarian sun can be intense, so prioritize sun protection. Pack sunscreen with a high SPF, a wide-brimmed hat to shade your face and neck, and sunglasses to protect your eyes from harmful UV rays.
>
> **Reusable Water Bottle:** Staying hydrated is crucial, especially when exploring La Palma's outdoors. A reusable water bottle is an eco-friendly and convenient way to carry water with you, reducing plastic waste and ensuring you have access to fresh water throughout the day.
>
> **Daypack or Backpack:** A small daypack or backpack is essential for carrying essentials during day trips, hikes, or excursions. Look for one with comfortable straps, multiple compartments for organization, and features like water bottle holders and rain covers for added convenience.

Accommodation Options
Luxury Hotels and Resorts

- **Parador de La Palma (Breña Baja)**

Nestled in the picturesque town of Breña Baja, Parador de La Palma is a charming hotel that exudes tranquility and elegance. Set within extensive grounds adorned with beautiful gardens, the hotel offers a peaceful retreat where guests can relax and connect with nature. The colonial-style architecture adds to the hotel's charm, with its elegant design and traditional Canarian elements creating a welcoming and nostalgic atmosphere. Parador de La Palma is known for its friendly service, comfortable accommodations, and a tranquil environment that invites relaxation and rejuvenation.

- **Hotel San Telmo (Santa Cruz de La Palma)**

Located in the heart of Santa Cruz de La Palma, the island's capital, Hotel San Telmo is a boutique hotel that seamlessly blends history and modern comfort. Housed in a beautifully converted 17th-century building, the hotel boasts impeccable style, with its architecture and interior design reflecting the island's rich heritage. Guests can expect personalized attention from the owners, who are passionate about providing a welcoming and memorable experience. The hotel's lovely breakfast, served in a charming setting, is a delightful way to start the day, and its central location provides easy access to the city's attractions, shops, and restaurants.

- **La Palma & Teneguía Princess Hotel (Fuencaliente)**

Situated on the sunny southwest coast of Fuencaliente, La Palma & Teneguía Princess Hotel offers a blend of traditional Canarian style and subtropical splendor. This beachfront hotel boasts one of the best swimming pool complexes in the archipelago, with a variety of pools, including an infinity pool with stunning ocean views, providing ample opportunities for relaxation and recreation. The hotel's spacious and comfortable rooms, combined with its excellent facilities and prime location, make it an ideal choice for couples and families seeking a tranquil getaway.

- **Hotel Benahoare (Los Llanos)**

In the heart of Los Llanos de Aridane, Hotel Benahoare is a smart and stylish hotel that offers excellent value for money. Its central location provides easy access to the town's shops, plazas, and restaurants, allowing guests to immerse themselves in the local atmosphere. The hotel features a stylish roof terrace with panoramic views, perfect for enjoying a drink or relaxing in the sunshine. The breakfast buffet is a highlight, offering a wide variety of fresh and local produce to start the day. Hotel Benahoare is also conveniently located near the Caldera de Taburiente National Park, making it an excellent base for hiking enthusiasts.

- **H10 Taburiente Playa (Los Cancajos)**

H10 Taburiente Playa is a friendly and characterful hotel located directly on the seafront in Los Cancajos, a charming coastal town. The hotel's comfortable rooms and prime location offer stunning sea views, allowing guests to wake up to the sound of waves and enjoy the beauty of the coastline. With its relaxed atmosphere and convenient access to the beach, H10 Taburiente Playa is perfect for those seeking a tranquil escape and the opportunity to connect with La Palma's natural beauty.

- **Hotel Valle Aridane (Valle Aridane)**

This 3-star hotel, located in the town of Valle Aridane, provides comfortable accommodations and a welcoming atmosphere. Known for its good service and convenient location, Hotel Valle

Aridane offers a pleasant and affordable base for exploring the island. The hotel's friendly staff is always ready to assist guests with their needs and provide recommendations for local attractions and activities.

- **Sombrero Pico 9 D**

Sombrero Pico 9 D is a hotel that prioritizes guest satisfaction, offering excellent service and comfortable accommodations. The hotel's well-appointed rooms provide a relaxing and welcoming environment, and the attentive staff ensures that guests feel well-cared for throughout their stay. Whether you're seeking a peaceful retreat or a base for exploring the island, Sombrero Pico 9 D provides a comfortable and enjoyable experience.

- **Finca Valentina**

Finca Valentina, a charming rural hotel located in the heart of La Palma, offers a peaceful escape from the hustle and bustle of everyday life. Surrounded by beautiful gardens and lush landscapes, the hotel provides a tranquil environment where guests can relax and reconnect with nature. The cozy atmosphere and personalized service create a welcoming and home-like experience. Finca Valentina is an ideal choice for those seeking a rural retreat and a chance to experience the authentic charm of La Palma.

- **Hacienda San Jorge**

Hacienda San Jorge is a luxury hotel that embodies elegance and sophistication. The hotel's spacious and elegantly decorated rooms provide a haven of comfort and style, while its extensive facilities cater to every need. Guests can unwind by the swimming pool, surrounded by lush gardens, or indulge in delectable local cuisine at the hotel's restaurant. Hacienda San Jorge is a perfect choice for those seeking a luxurious and pampered experience in La Palma.

- **Hotel Emblemático Holiday Time (Los Llanos)**

Located in the town of Los Llanos de Aridane, Hotel Emblemático Holiday Time offers comfortable accommodations and a convenient location for exploring the island. The hotel features a lovely garden, providing a tranquil oasis for relaxation, and its proximity to local attractions, shops, and restaurants makes it an ideal base for exploring the surrounding area.

Budget-Friendly Stays

- **Hotel Valle Aridane (Valle Aridane)**

Located in the town of Valle Aridane, this 3-star hotel offers a pleasant and affordable stay in La Palma. The hotel's comfortable rooms provide a welcoming retreat after a day of exploring the island's attractions. With its friendly service and convenient location, Hotel Valle Aridane is a great base for discovering the natural beauty and cultural heritage of La Palma.

- **Finca Cosmos (Breña Baja)**

Nestled in the charming town of Breña Baja, Finca Cosmos offers cozy accommodations with a touch of rustic charm. The hotel features a lovely garden, where guests can relax and enjoy the tranquil atmosphere. Its proximity to the beach makes it an ideal choice for those seeking a budget-friendly stay with easy access to the coast. Finca Cosmos provides a comfortable and welcoming environment for travelers seeking a relaxed and affordable La Palma experience.

- **Oasis San Antonio (Barlovento)**

Located in the northern part of La Palma, Oasis San Antonio is a small and intimate hotel with only 10 rooms. This charming hotel offers a peaceful and tranquil atmosphere, ideal for those seeking an escape from the hustle and bustle of everyday life. Its location within the Biosphere Reserve of Barlovento provides easy access to the area's natural beauty, with hiking trails, lush forests, and stunning coastal views. Oasis San Antonio is a perfect choice for nature lovers and those seeking a quiet and affordable retreat.

- **Apartamentos Adjovimar (Los Llanos)**

Apartamentos Adjovimar, located in the town of Los Llanos de Aridane, offers a convenient and comfortable stay for budget-conscious travelers. The apartments are situated near the bus station, providing easy access to public transportation and making it convenient to explore the west side of the island. With their well-equipped kitchens and comfortable living spaces, these apartments offer a home-away-from-home experience for those seeking an independent and affordable stay.

- **El Cerrito (Breña Alta)**

El Cerrito, a charming hotel in the town of Breña Alta, offers a peaceful and budget-friendly retreat. The hotel's comfortable rooms and lovely garden provide a relaxing environment for guests to unwind and enjoy the tranquility of La Palma. Its location in Breña Alta offers easy access to the town's attractions, as well as the surrounding natural beauty of the island.

- **Hotel La Posada (Central La Palma)**

Situated in the center of La Palma, Hotel La Posada provides simple yet comfortable accommodations at an affordable price. The hotel features a café-bar, where guests can enjoy a drink or a light meal, and offers free Wi-Fi access, making it a convenient choice for travelers who need to stay connected. Hotel La Posada's central location provides easy access to the island's attractions and transportation hubs.

- **Apartamentos Turísticos Puerta Real (Near La Palma)**

Located near La Palma, Apartamentos Turísticos Puerta Real offers spacious and modern accommodations for budget-conscious travelers. The apartments are well-equipped with all the necessary amenities for a comfortable stay, including kitchens, living areas, and private balconies. With their excellent value for money and convenient location, these apartments are a popular choice for those seeking an independent and affordable stay.

- **Alojamiento Vacacional El Vinagrillo (Cartagena)**

Alojamiento Vacacional El Vinagrillo, located in Cartagena near La Palma, offers comfortable and affordable accommodations with convenient amenities. The air-conditioned rooms provide a welcome respite from the warm climate, and the availability of parking makes it a convenient choice for those traveling by car. This accommodation is a great option for budget-conscious travelers seeking a comfortable and hassle-free stay.

- **Vivienda con Parking en el Centro de Cartagena (Cartagena)**

This centrally located house in Cartagena offers a budget-friendly stay with a touch of home comfort. With its convenient location, guests have easy access to local shops, restaurants, and attractions. The house provides a comfortable and affordable base for exploring the surrounding area and experiencing the local culture.

Unique Lodging Experiences

- **Ecofinca Luna (Tijarafe)**

Ecofinca Luna is an eco-friendly farm stay nestled in the municipality of Tijarafe, offering a unique opportunity to experience sustainable living and connect with nature. This off-the-grid property utilizes solar power and water-saving systems, minimizing its environmental impact and showcasing a harmonious relationship with the surrounding environment.

Accommodations at Ecofinca Luna range from charming cottages to glamping tents, all thoughtfully designed and furnished with eco-friendly materials. The property is set amidst lush gardens and orchards, where guests can participate in farm activities, such as harvesting vegetables, learning about permaculture practices, and experiencing the daily rhythms of sustainable living. Ecofinca Luna is an ideal choice for environmentally conscious travelers seeking an authentic and immersive experience in La Palma's natural beauty.

- **El Castaño Encantado (Garafía)**

Nestled in the heart of the Garafía region, El Castaño Encantado is a rural retreat that offers a truly magical experience. Surrounded by a canopy of chestnut trees, the property provides a tranquil escape from the hustle and bustle of everyday life. Guests can choose from a selection of rustic cabins and treehouses, each designed to blend seamlessly with the natural environment and offer a unique perspective of the forest.

The cabins and treehouses at El Castaño Encantado are crafted with natural materials and feature cozy interiors that evoke a sense of warmth and tranquility. Guests can relax on private balconies, listen to the sounds of nature, and enjoy the serenity of the surrounding forest. This unique lodging experience is perfect for those seeking to reconnect with nature and experience the magic of La Palma's forests.

- **Casa El Morro (Tazacorte)**

Casa El Morro is a beautifully restored 17th-century Canarian house located in the quaint village of Tazacorte. This historic property offers a blend of traditional architecture and modern comforts, providing a unique glimpse into La Palma's rich cultural heritage. Guests can stay in individually decorated rooms that reflect the island's history and artistic traditions.

The house features a charming courtyard, where guests can relax and enjoy the tranquil atmosphere, as well as a small pool for refreshing dips. The stunning views of the surrounding landscapes, including the majestic volcanic peaks and the sparkling Atlantic Ocean, add to the allure of this historic haven. Casa El Morro is an ideal choice for history enthusiasts and those seeking an authentic Canarian experience.

- **La Hilera del Laurel (El Paso)**

La Hilera del Laurel, located in the town of El Paso, offers a truly unique lodging experience: the chance to stay in traditional Canarian cave houses. These cave accommodations, carved into the volcanic rock, are naturally insulated, providing a comfortable and cozy stay year-round.

The cave houses at La Hilera del Laurel are beautifully furnished and equipped with modern amenities, while retaining their rustic charm and connection to the island's volcanic origins. Guests can enjoy the unique ambiance of these cave dwellings, relax in the tranquil surroundings, and admire the stunning views of the Caldera de Taburiente National Park. The nearby hiking trails offer opportunities to explore the island's natural beauty and discover hidden corners of this volcanic landscape.

- **El Sitio (Villa de Mazo):**

El Sitio, located in the town of Villa de Mazo, is a sustainable retreat that offers a range of unique and eco-friendly accommodations. Guests can choose from yurts, traditional Mongolian tents that provide a nomadic experience; geodesic domes, modern structures that blend seamlessly with the natural environment; and traditional Canarian houses, restored to their original charm while incorporating sustainable practices.

Each accommodation at El Sitio is thoughtfully designed to minimize its environmental impact, utilizing renewable energy sources and water-saving systems. The property features organic gardens, where guests can learn about sustainable agriculture and enjoy fresh produce, as well as a communal kitchen for preparing meals and connecting with fellow travelers. A wellness area offers yoga and meditation sessions, providing opportunities for relaxation and rejuvenation.

- **Finca La Principal (Aridane Valley)**

Finca La Principal is a beautiful estate located in the fertile Aridane Valley, offering a luxurious and authentic rural experience. This historic property, dating back to the 19th century, features a selection of elegantly restored farmhouses that blend traditional architecture with modern comforts.

Guests can enjoy the serene surroundings, which include vineyards, orchards, and lush gardens, providing a tranquil escape from the everyday hustle. The finca also offers guided tours of the property, allowing guests to learn about the history of the estate, the agricultural practices of the region, and the unique characteristics of La Palma's landscape. Finca La Principal is an ideal choice for those seeking a luxurious yet authentic rural experience, where history, nature, and comfort intertwine.

- **La Posada de Tazacorte (Tazacorte)**

La Posada de Tazacorte, a boutique hotel housed in a former banana plantation house in the village of Tazacorte, offers a unique blend of history and modern comfort. The hotel's stylish accommodations feature a touch of colonial elegance, reflecting the island's rich past and its connection to the banana trade that once thrived in the region.

Guests can relax in the hotel's beautiful garden, take a refreshing dip in the swimming pool, or savor local cuisine at the on-site restaurant. The terrace offers stunning views of the Atlantic Ocean and the surrounding countryside, providing a picturesque setting for enjoying a meal or simply unwinding with a drink.

- **Fuencaliente Lighthouse**

For a truly unique and unforgettable experience, consider staying at the Fuencaliente Lighthouse. This historic lighthouse, located on the southern tip of La Palma, has been converted into a charming guesthouse, offering a remote and tranquil escape.

The accommodations at the Fuencaliente Lighthouse provide breathtaking views of the ocean and the rugged coastline, allowing guests to immerse themselves in the island's natural beauty. The surrounding volcanic landscape, with its lava flows and volcanic cones, offers opportunities for exploration and adventure. Guests can also visit the nearby salt flats, where traditional methods are used to harvest sea salt, and experience the unique ecosystem of this coastal region.

- **Hacienda de Abajo (Tazacorte)**

Hacienda de Abajo, a luxury hotel located in the historic town of Tazacorte, offers a unique blend of history, elegance, and modern comfort. This former sugar plantation has been meticulously restored and transformed into a luxurious hotel, with beautifully landscaped gardens, a spa offering rejuvenating treatments, and a gourmet restaurant serving exquisite cuisine.

Each room at Hacienda de Abajo is uniquely decorated with antiques and artwork, reflecting the rich cultural heritage of La Palma and creating an ambiance of refined elegance. The hotel's attention to detail and commitment to preserving the property's historical character make it a truly special place to stay.

- **La Palma Yoga Retreat (Puntagorda)**

Located in the serene town of Puntagorda, La Palma Yoga Retreat offers a holistic lodging experience focused on wellness and rejuvenation. The retreat features a variety of accommodations, including cozy cabins and luxurious suites, all designed to provide a comfortable and tranquil environment for guests to relax and reconnect with themselves.

Guests can participate in daily yoga and meditation sessions, led by experienced instructors, to enhance their physical and mental well-being. Healthy vegetarian meals, prepared with fresh, local ingredients, nourish the body and support a balanced lifestyle. The retreat's beautiful surroundings, with its peaceful gardens and stunning views, provide the perfect backdrop for relaxation and introspection.

Exploring Santa Cruz de La Palma
Historical Landmarks

Santa Cruz de La Palma
Santa Cruz de La Palma, the vibrant capital of La Palma, is a treasure trove of history, culture, and architectural beauty. Founded in 1493 by the Spanish conquistador Alonso Fernández de Lugo, the city has witnessed centuries of fascinating events and transformations, leaving behind a legacy of charming streets, colonial-style buildings, and a rich cultural heritage.

Exploring the Historic Old Town
The old town of Santa Cruz de La Palma is a delight to explore, with its narrow cobblestone streets, colorful houses adorned with carved wooden balconies, and a relaxed atmosphere that invites leisurely strolls. The city's historic center is a testament to its colonial past, with well-preserved buildings that reflect the architectural styles of the 16th and 17th centuries.

> **A Fusion of Architectural Styles:** The architecture of Santa Cruz de La Palma showcases a blend of Canarian, Spanish, and Flemish influences, reflecting the island's diverse history and its connections with Europe. The traditional Canarian houses, with their whitewashed walls, wooden balconies, and red-tiled roofs, create a charming and picturesque ambiance.

> **Religious Art and History:** The city's churches are not only places of worship but also repositories of artistic treasures. Many of them house significant collections of Flemish religious art, showcasing exquisite paintings and sculptures that reflect the island's historical ties with Flanders. The Insular Museum, located in a former Franciscan convent, complements the city's artistic

heritage with its remarkable collection of paintings, sculptures, and artifacts that tell the story of La Palma's cultural evolution.

Landmarks of History and Culture
Santa Cruz de La Palma boasts several landmarks that offer glimpses into the island's rich history and cultural heritage.

Castle of Santa Catalina: Standing proudly on Avenida Marítima, the Castle of Santa Catalina is a historic-artistic monument that dates back to the 16th century. Built to protect the city from pirate attacks, the castle's sturdy walls and strategic location played a crucial role in defending the island during a turbulent era. The castle's walls were reinforced after a famous siege by the French privateer François Le Clerc in 1553, an event that is still commemorated in the city today. Visitors can explore the castle's ramparts, admire the views of the city and the sea, and delve into the island's defensive history.

Salazar Palace: Erected in the 17th century, Salazar Palace is a magnificent example of noble architecture, reflecting the wealth and influence of the merchants who once resided in Santa Cruz de La Palma. Built by wealthy families from Flanders who settled on the island, the palace is a testament to La Palma's rich commercial history and its connections with Europe. The palace's elegant design and intricate details showcase the architectural prowess of the period and offer a glimpse into the lifestyle of the island's elite.

Churches of Artistic Significance: Santa Cruz de La Palma is home to several churches that not only serve as places of worship but also house remarkable collections of religious art.

Church of El Salvador: This church is renowned for its important Flemish carvings and artworks, showcasing the island's historical and artistic connections with Flanders. The church's interior is adorned with intricate wood carvings and paintings that reflect the influence of Flemish artistic traditions on the island.

Church of Santo Domingo: Another church with a rich artistic heritage, the Church of Santo Domingo houses a significant collection of paintings from the Canary Islands, showcasing the talent and creativity of local artists. The church's interior is a testament to the island's artistic legacy and its connections with the broader artistic movements of the time.

Church of San Francisco: The Church of San Francisco features a remarkable wood carving of "Santa Ana, the Virgin and Child," a masterpiece of Flemish craftsmanship that reflects the island's historical ties with Flanders. The church's interior is adorned with beautiful wood carvings and paintings, showcasing the island's artistic traditions and its appreciation for religious art.

Cultural Influences and Historical Events

Santa Cruz de La Palma's history is interwoven with the influence of families from Flanders and Ireland who settled on the island during its colonial era. Many of the city's iconic buildings, such as the Salazar Palace, were built by these merchants, and their influence can still be seen in the city's architecture and cultural heritage.

The Mark of the Flemish and the Irish: The presence of Flemish and Irish families in Santa Cruz de La Palma has left a lasting impact on the city's identity. Their contributions to the island's economy, architecture, and culture are still evident today. The city's historic center reflects the architectural styles and traditions brought by these settlers, creating a unique blend of Canarian and European influences.

The Ship Santa Maria: Located at the northern exit of the city, the representation of the ship Santa Maria is a reminder of La Palma's historical connection with the Americas. The ship, a replica of one of Christopher Columbus's vessels, symbolizes the island's role in the Age of Exploration and its maritime heritage.

The Day of the Corsair: Every August, Santa Cruz de La Palma commemorates a significant historical event with the Day of the Corsair. This lively reenactment of the famous pirate attack by François Le Clerc in 1553 brings the city's history to life. The event includes dramatized performances by young people from the island, musical performances, and a festive atmosphere that captures the spirit of this historical event.

Museums and Galleries

La Palma, the "Beautiful Island," is not only a place of stunning landscapes and natural wonders but also a treasure trove of cultural and scientific knowledge. The island's museums and cultural centers offer fascinating insights into its history, traditions, and natural environment, providing visitors with a deeper understanding of La Palma's unique identity.

Delving into the Past

La Palma's museums offer a captivating journey through time, unveiling the island's rich history and the diverse cultures that have shaped its identity.

> **Museo Arqueologico Benahoarita (Los Llanos de Aridane):** This museum is dedicated to preserving and showcasing the heritage of the Benahoaritas, the original inhabitants of La Palma. The museum's collection includes a fascinating array of archaeological artifacts, such as pottery, tools, jewelry, and skeletal remains, providing a glimpse into the daily life, customs, and beliefs of these indigenous people. Visitors can learn about the Benahoaritas' unique culture, their connection to the island's environment, and their legacy in La Palma's history.
>
> **Museo Insular de La Palma (Santa Cruz de La Palma):** The Insular Museum of La Palma offers a comprehensive overview of the island's history, culture, and natural environment. Housed in a beautifully restored 16th-century building, the museum features a diverse range of exhibits that cover various aspects of La Palma's heritage. Visitors can explore the island's natural history, including its volcanic origins, unique flora and fauna, and geological formations. The museum also showcases the island's

artistic traditions, with exhibits on painting, sculpture, and traditional crafts. Additionally, the museum delves into the island's ethnography, showcasing the customs, traditions, and social history of its people.

Celebrating La Palma's Unique Traditions and Industries

La Palma's museums also celebrate the island's unique traditions, agricultural heritage, and craftsmanship.

Museo del Plátano de Tazacorte (Tazacorte): This museum is dedicated to the history and cultivation of bananas on La Palma, highlighting the significant role that this fruit has played in the island's economy and culture. The museum's exhibits explore the agricultural practices, processing methods, and economic impact of banana farming in La Palma. Visitors can learn about the journey of the banana from plantation to market, the challenges faced by banana growers, and the importance of this industry to the island's livelihood.

Museo de Interpretación del Gofio (MIGO) (Garafia): Gofio, a traditional Canarian flour made from roasted grains, holds a special place in La Palma's culinary heritage. The Museo de Interpretación del Gofio (MIGO) in Garafia is dedicated to exploring the history and cultural significance of this staple food. The museum provides information on the production process, nutritional benefits, and traditional recipes, showcasing the versatility and importance of gofio in Canarian cuisine.

Museo de la Seda Las Hilanderas (El Paso): The Museo de la Seda Las Hilanderas celebrates the art of silk production, a traditional craft that once thrived on La Palma. The museum showcases the intricate process of silk weaving, spinning, and dyeing, offering visitors a glimpse into the skills and artistry involved in creating these exquisite textiles. The museum also features demonstrations and workshops, allowing visitors to learn about the different stages of silk production and even try their hand at some of the techniques.

Maritime History and Religious Art

La Palma's museums also delve into the island's maritime history and religious heritage, showcasing its connections to the wider world and its spiritual traditions.

Museo Naval - Barco de la Virgen (Santa Cruz de La Palma): This unique museum, housed in a building shaped like a ship, is dedicated to the maritime history of the Canary Islands. The museum's exhibits explore various aspects of maritime life, including shipbuilding techniques, navigation methods, and the role of the Canary Islands in maritime trade routes. Visitors can learn about the island's historical connections with Europe, Africa, and the Americas, and the impact of maritime trade on La Palma's development.

Museo Camarín de Las Nieves (Santa Cruz de La Palma): Housed in a former convent, the Museo Camarín de Las Nieves features a collection of religious art, including paintings, sculptures, and artifacts from La Palma's religious history. The museum's collection reflects the island's strong Catholic traditions and the influence of religious art on its cultural heritage. Visitors can admire the intricate details of religious artworks, learn about the stories and symbolism behind them, and gain a deeper understanding of La Palma's spiritual life.

Volcanic Landscapes and Astronomical Wonders

La Palma's museums also showcase the island's unique volcanic landscapes and its position as a leading center for astronomical research.

Centro de Visitantes del Volcán de San Antonio: Located near the San Antonio volcano, this visitor center provides a fascinating glimpse into La Palma's volcanic activity. The center's exhibits offer information on volcanic eruptions, lava flows, and the formation of the island's dramatic landscapes. Visitors can learn about the science behind volcanoes, the history of volcanic activity on La Palma, and the ongoing monitoring efforts to understand and mitigate volcanic hazards.

Centro de Visitantes de La Caldera de Taburiente: Situated at the entrance to the Caldera de Taburiente National Park, this visitor center offers a comprehensive introduction to the park's natural wonders. The center features exhibits on the park's geological formation, diverse flora and fauna, and the importance of conservation efforts to protect this unique ecosystem. Visitors can learn about the park's hiking trails, plan their explorations, and gain a deeper appreciation for the natural beauty and biodiversity of La Palma.

Instituto de Astrofísica de Canarias (Roque de los Muchachos Observatory): La Palma is renowned for its clear skies and minimal light pollution, making it an ideal location for astronomical observation. The Instituto de Astrofísica de Canarias, located at the Roque de los Muchachos Observatory, offers public tours and exhibits on astronomy and astrophysics. Visitors can learn about the cutting-edge research conducted at the observatory, explore the fascinating world of stars and galaxies, and even have the opportunity to observe the night sky through powerful telescopes.

Natural Wonders and Outdoor Activities
La Caldera de Taburiente National Park

Geological Formation and History
La Caldera de Taburiente is not a volcano in the traditional sense, but rather a massive depression formed by a combination of volcanic activity and erosion. The caldera, measuring approximately 10 kilometers in diameter and plunging to depths of 2000 meters, resembles a vast amphitheater carved into the island's heart.

The formation of the caldera began millions of years ago with intense volcanic eruptions and tectonic shifts that shaped the island's early landscape. Over time, erosion played a crucial role in sculpting the caldera's dramatic features, with water carving deep ravines and shaping the towering cliffs that define its boundaries.

The park was officially declared a National Park in 1954, recognizing its unique geological and ecological significance and ensuring the protection of its diverse ecosystems and natural beauty.

Flora and Fauna
La Caldera de Taburiente National Park is a biodiversity hotspot, home to a remarkable variety of plant and animal life, many of which are endemic to the Canary Islands.

>   **Forests of Laurisilva and Pine:** The park's varied microclimates and altitudes support a range of vegetation types. In the higher, more humid areas, lush laurel forests, known as "laurisilva," thrive. These ancient forests are

remnants of the subtropical forests that once covered much of Southern Europe and North Africa, and they harbor a unique collection of plant species, including the Canary Island laurel, fern trees, and holly. Lower down, the landscape transitions to Canary Island pine forests, which are adapted to the volcanic soils and possess a remarkable resistance to fire, playing a crucial role in the island's ecosystem.

Avian Diversity: The park's diverse habitats support a rich variety of birdlife. The endemic Bolle's pigeon and the Laurel pigeon, with their distinctive calls and colorful plumage, can often be spotted in the laurel forests. Birds of prey, such as the Barbary falcon and the long-eared owl, soar through the skies, while smaller birds, like the Canary Island chiffchaff and the blue chaffinch, flit among the trees.

Reptiles and Aquatic Life: Reptiles, including the Tenerife lizard and various species of geckos, are common sights in the park, basking in the sun on rocks or camouflaged among the vegetation. The park's streams and rivers support a variety of freshwater fish, adding to the biodiversity of this unique ecosystem.

Hiking and Outdoor Activities

La Caldera de Taburiente National Park is a hiker's paradise, offering a network of well-maintained trails that cater to all levels of experience.

Trails for Every Level: Whether you're seeking a leisurely stroll or a challenging trek, the park has a trail to suit your needs. One of the most famous routes is the Ruta de la Crestería, which follows the rim of the caldera, offering breathtaking panoramic views of the surrounding landscapes, including the towering cliffs, deep ravines, and volcanic peaks. Another popular trail is the Barranco de las Angustias, which descends into the heart of the caldera, passing through lush vegetation and alongside the Taburiente River, providing a more intimate experience of the park's natural beauty.

Roque de los Muchachos: For those seeking a more challenging adventure, the Roque de los Muchachos is a must-visit. This peak, the highest point on La Palma, stands at 2426 meters and is located on the rim of the caldera. The views from the Roque de los Muchachos are simply breathtaking, encompassing the entire island, the neighboring Canary Islands, and the vast expanse of the Atlantic Ocean. The area is also home to the Roque de los Muchachos Observatory, one of the world's leading astronomical observatories, where visitors can learn about the park's exceptionally dark skies and the importance of astronomical research.

Waterfalls and Natural Pools
The park is adorned with numerous waterfalls and natural pools, adding to its enchanting beauty and providing refreshing escapes from the summer heat.

Cascada de la Desfondada: This spectacular waterfall, cascading 150 meters down a steep cliff face, is a testament to the power of erosion and the beauty of La Palma's natural forces. The waterfall's dramatic plunge into a deep ravine creates a mesmerizing spectacle that captivates visitors.

Cascada de Los Colores: The Cascada de Los Colores, or Waterfall of Colors, is a unique natural wonder named for the vibrant hues created by mineral deposits in the water. The waterfall's striking colors, ranging from reds and oranges to yellows and greens, create a visual feast for the eyes and make it a popular spot for photographers and nature enthusiasts.

Natural Pools: The park's rivers and streams have carved out natural pools, offering refreshing spots for a swim during the warmer months. The Taburiente Pool, located in the heart of the caldera, is a tranquil oasis surrounded by lush vegetation and towering cliffs. These natural pools provide a serene setting for relaxation and contemplation, allowing visitors to connect with the park's natural beauty.

Cultural and Historical Significance

La Caldera de Taburiente holds deep cultural and historical significance for the people of La Palma. The island's indigenous inhabitants, the Benahoaritas, revered the caldera as a sacred place, believing it to be the dwelling place of their gods. Archaeological sites within the park, including rock carvings and ancient artifacts, provide glimpses into the lives of these early inhabitants and their connection to the land.

The caldera also played a role in the Spanish conquest of La Palma in the 15th century. The Benahoaritas sought refuge in the caldera's rugged terrain, using its natural defenses to resist the Spanish invaders. Remnants of their defensive structures can still be found within the park, serving as reminders of the island's history and the resilience of its indigenous people.

Conservation Efforts

Conservation is a key priority in La Caldera de Taburiente National Park. The park's management is dedicated to protecting its unique ecosystems, biodiversity, and geological formations for future generations. Efforts include reforestation projects to restore native vegetation, invasive species control to protect the delicate balance of the ecosystem, and the preservation of water resources to ensure the long-term health of the park.

Education and outreach programs play a vital role in raising awareness about the importance of conservation and promoting sustainable tourism practices. Visitors are encouraged to respect the park's natural environment, stay on marked trails, and minimize their impact on the delicate ecosystem.

Visitor Information
La Caldera de Taburiente National Park is accessible year-round, but the best times to visit are during the spring and autumn when the weather is mild and the landscapes are at their most vibrant. The Visitor Center in El Paso provides comprehensive information about the park, including maps, trail guides, and exhibits on the park's geology, flora, and fauna. Guided tours are available for those who wish to learn more about the park's natural and cultural history from knowledgeable local guides.

Volcano Hiking Trails
- **Ruta de los Volcanes (Volcano Route)**

The Ruta de los Volcanes is arguably La Palma's most iconic and challenging hiking trail. This 17-kilometer route takes hikers on a journey through the island's volcanic heart, traversing a series of volcanic cones and craters in the southern part of the island.

Starting from the town of El Pilar, the trail ascends through the Cumbre Vieja mountain range, offering breathtaking views of the surrounding landscapes. Hikers will encounter the Teneguía Volcano, the youngest volcano on the island, which last erupted in 1971, leaving behind a rugged and otherworldly terrain. The trail also passes by the San Antonio Volcano, known for its impressive crater and panoramic views of the island's southern coastline.

The Ruta de los Volcanes concludes in the town of Fuencaliente, where hikers can explore the Fuencaliente Salt Pans, a unique ecosystem where seawater is evaporated to produce sea salt, and enjoy the stunning coastal scenery. This challenging hike is a testament to La Palma's volcanic origins and offers a rewarding experience for those seeking adventure and breathtaking views.

- **Volcano San Antonio and Teneguía**

For those seeking a shorter but equally impressive volcanic hike, the Volcano San Antonio and Teneguía trail provides a captivating experience. This route begins at the visitor center near the San Antonio Volcano, where hikers can learn about the island's volcanic history and geology through informative exhibits and displays. The trail then ascends to the crater of the San Antonio Volcano, offering spectacular views of the surrounding landscape, including the neighboring Teneguía Volcano and the vast expanse of the Atlantic Ocean. Continuing on, hikers will reach the Teneguía Volcano, where they can explore its rugged terrain and witness the stark beauty of this young volcanic landscape.

The hike concludes with a descent to the coastal village of Fuencaliente, where hikers can relax and enjoy the charming atmosphere of this traditional Canarian town.

- **Volcán de San Juan**

The Volcán de San Juan trail offers a fascinating glimpse into La Palma's volcanic history. Located in the central part of the island, the trail starts near the town of Las Manchas and takes hikers through lush pine forests and past the San Juan Volcano, which erupted in 1949.

The eruption of the San Juan Volcano created a dramatic landscape of lava flows and volcanic cones, which are still visible today, providing a unique perspective on the island's geological processes. The trail also passes by the Llano del Jable viewpoint, offering stunning panoramic views of the surrounding mountains, valleys, and the vast expanse of the Caldera de Taburiente National Park. This moderate hike is a great way to explore the island's natural beauty and volcanic heritage.

- **Cumbre Vieja Ridge**

The Cumbre Vieja Ridge trail offers an exhilarating hike along one of La Palma's most prominent volcanic features. Starting from the Refugio del Pilar, a mountain hut that provides basic accommodation and refreshments, the trail follows the crest of the Cumbre Vieja mountain range, passing by numerous volcanic craters and cones.

This challenging hike covers approximately 24 kilometers and provides hikers with stunning panoramic views of the island's diverse landscapes, from lush forests and deep ravines to volcanic peaks and the vast expanse of the Atlantic Ocean. Key highlights along the trail include the Deseada Volcano, the highest point of the Cumbre Vieja, and the Nambroque Volcano, known for its unique lava formations. The trail ends in the town of Los Canarios, where hikers can relax and reflect on their journey.

- **Ruta de los Dragos**

The Ruta de los Dragos is a scenic hike that combines the beauty of volcanic landscapes with the lush greenery of ancient forests and the unique presence of dragon trees. This trail begins in the village of Puntallana and follows a path through the Barranco del Agua gorge, a deep ravine carved by water erosion.

Hikers will pass by the Los Dragos forest, home to a unique population of dragon trees, which are endemic to the Canary Islands and hold cultural and historical significance. The trail then ascends to the Caldereta volcano, offering breathtaking views of the surrounding valleys and the Atlantic Ocean. This moderate hike provides a perfect blend of natural beauty, volcanic history, and botanical wonders.

- **Nambroque and Hoyo Negro**

For experienced hikers seeking a challenging adventure, the Nambroque and Hoyo Negro trail offers an unforgettable experience. This strenuous hike starts from the Refugio del Pilar and follows a steep path up to the Nambroque Volcano, requiring a good level of fitness and hiking experience.

The ascent is rewarded with panoramic views of the Cumbre Vieja mountain range and the surrounding landscapes, showcasing the island's volcanic grandeur. The trail then continues to the Hoyo Negro crater, a striking volcanic feature formed by a powerful eruption in 1949. The crater's deep depression and rugged terrain create an otherworldly atmosphere. The hike concludes with a descent to the town of Los Canarios.

- **Volcano Bejenao**

The Volcano Bejenao trail is a popular hike that offers stunning views of the Caldera de Taburiente National Park. Starting from the area known as La Cumbrecita, the trail ascends through lush pine forests to the summit of the Bejenao Volcano, providing a challenging but rewarding experience.

The hike offers panoramic views of the caldera, with its towering cliffs and deep ravines, as well as the surrounding mountains and the vast expanse of the Atlantic Ocean. Along the way, hikers can enjoy the diverse flora and fauna that inhabit the park, including endemic species of plants and birds.

Beaches and Natural Pools

- **Playa de Puerto Naos**

Playa de Puerto Naos, located on the west coast of La Palma, is a beloved destination for both locals and tourists. This expansive black sand beach, framed by swaying palm trees, offers a picturesque setting for enjoying the island's coastal beauty. The beach's calm, crystal-clear waters are ideal for swimming, snorkeling, and exploring the underwater world.

Puerto Naos is also a popular spot for paragliding, thanks to its favorable wind conditions. The sight of colorful paragliders soaring above the beach adds to the vibrant atmosphere. The beach is well-equipped with amenities, including sunbeds, umbrellas, and a variety of restaurants and bars where visitors can enjoy refreshments and local cuisine while soaking in the stunning ocean views.

- **Playa de Tazacorte**

Situated in the historic town of Tazacorte, Playa de Tazacorte is another beautiful black sand beach that offers a diverse range of experiences. The beach is divided into two distinct sections, catering to different preferences.

The first section is a family-friendly area with calm waters, perfect for swimming and enjoying water activities with children. The gentle waves and shallow waters provide a safe and enjoyable environment for families to relax and have fun.

The second section of Playa de Tazacorte is more rugged and exposed to the open ocean, attracting surfers and bodyboarders who seek the thrill of riding the waves. The powerful waves and dynamic currents create an exciting playground for water sports enthusiasts.

The promenade that runs along the beach is lined with colorful buildings, adding to the town's charm. A variety of restaurants and cafes offer delicious dining options, where visitors can savor fresh seafood and local specialties while enjoying the stunning sunset views over the Atlantic Ocean.

- **Playa de Nogales**

Playa de Nogales, located on the northern coast near Puntallana, is considered one of the most stunning and unspoiled beaches on La Palma. This secluded beach is nestled amidst dramatic cliffs and lush vegetation, creating a sense of tranquility and natural beauty.

Reaching Playa de Nogales involves a scenic hike down the cliffs, adding an element of adventure to the experience. The beach's black volcanic sand and powerful waves make it a popular spot for surfers, while the tranquil atmosphere and breathtaking scenery attract those seeking a peaceful escape.

- **Playa de Echentive**

Playa de Echentive, located in the southern part of the island near Fuencaliente, is a relatively new beach formed by volcanic activity from the Teneguía eruption in 1971. This unique beach features black sand and volcanic rock formations, creating a striking and otherworldly landscape.

The clear waters of Playa de Echentive are ideal for snorkeling, allowing visitors to explore the underwater volcanic terrain and discover the marine life that thrives in this environment. The beach's relative isolation and rugged beauty provide a peaceful and serene escape for those seeking a unique coastal experience.

- **Charco Azul**

Charco Azul, located in the municipality of San Andrés y Sauces, is one of La Palma's most famous natural pools. This series of saltwater pools, formed by volcanic rock, offers a safe and calm swimming experience, sheltered from the waves of the Atlantic Ocean.

The pools vary in size and depth, making them suitable for all ages and swimming abilities. Charco Azul is well-maintained, with facilities including changing rooms, sunbathing areas, and a small restaurant where visitors can enjoy refreshments and local cuisine. The stunning views of the rugged coastline and the refreshing waters of the pools make Charco Azul a must-visit destination.

- **Playa de Los Cancajos**

Located near the capital city of Santa Cruz de La Palma, Playa de Los Cancajos is a popular beach destination known for its black sand and excellent snorkeling opportunities. The beach is sheltered by natural rock formations, creating calm and safe swimming conditions for families and individuals.

The waters surrounding Playa de Los Cancajos are teeming with marine life, making it a favorite spot for snorkelers and divers who wish to explore the underwater world. The beach is well-equipped with amenities, including sunbeds, showers, and a variety of restaurants and bars along the promenade, offering a convenient and enjoyable beach experience.

- **Playa de La Zamora**

Playa de La Zamora, located on the southwestern coast near Fuencaliente, is a secluded beach divided into two sections: La Zamora Grande and La Zamora Chica. Both sections feature black volcanic sand and are surrounded by dramatic cliffs, creating a sense of isolation and natural beauty.

The beach is known for its clear waters and abundant marine life, making it a great spot for snorkeling and exploring the underwater world. Due to its remote location, La Zamora offers a tranquil and uncrowded environment, perfect for those seeking peace and solitude amidst stunning natural scenery.

- **Piscinas de La Fajana**

The natural pools at La Fajana, located in the northern part of the island near Barlovento, are another fantastic spot for swimming and relaxation. These pools, formed by volcanic rock and filled with seawater, provide a safe and enjoyable swimming experience for all ages.

The pools vary in size and depth, catering to both adults and children. The surrounding area is equipped with sunbathing platforms, picnic areas, and a small restaurant, offering a convenient and comfortable environment for visitors. The rugged coastline and crashing waves create a dramatic backdrop, adding to the allure of La Fajana.

- **Playa de Las Monjas**

Playa de Las Monjas, also known as Playa de Las Mujeres, is a hidden gem located in the western part of the island near Tazacorte. This secluded beach is accessible via a hiking trail that winds through lush vegetation and volcanic rock formations, adding an element of adventure to the experience.

The beach features black sand and clear waters, making it an ideal spot for swimming and snorkeling. The secluded nature of Playa de Las Monjas ensures a peaceful and uncrowded environment, perfect for those seeking tranquility and a connection with nature.

- **Playa de Bajamar**

Playa de Bajamar, located near the town of Breña Alta, is a charming beach known for its fine black sand and calm waters. The gentle waves and shallow waters make it a great spot for families with children, offering a safe and enjoyable environment for swimming and playing.

The beach is equipped with amenities, including showers, sunbeds, and a small kiosk for refreshments. The nearby promenade offers a variety of dining options where you can enjoy local cuisine while overlooking the ocean. Bajamar's tranquil atmosphere and beautiful surroundings make it a favorite among locals and visitors seeking a relaxing beach experience.

Stargazing and Astronomical Tourism

La Palma, the "Beautiful Island," is not only renowned for its stunning landscapes and volcanic wonders but also for its exceptional stargazing opportunities. The island's commitment to preserving its dark skies, combined with its high altitude and favorable atmospheric conditions, has made it a world-leading destination for astronomical observation and astrotourism.

The Canary Islands' Skies

The Canary Islands, including La Palma, are recognized as some of the best locations in the world for observing the night sky. The clarity and darkness of the skies above La Palma are protected by law, ensuring minimal light pollution and optimal conditions for astronomical observation.

The Law of the Sky, enacted in 1988, regulates outdoor lighting across the island to minimize light pollution and preserve the pristine darkness of the night sky. This pioneering legislation has helped to create an environment where stars and celestial objects can be observed with exceptional clarity, attracting astronomers, astrophotographers, and stargazing enthusiasts from around the globe.

Roque de los Muchachos Observatory
One of the most significant attractions for astrotourism in La Palma is the Roque de los Muchachos Observatory. Perched at an altitude of 2426 meters on the edge of the Caldera de Taburiente National Park, this observatory is a world-leading center for astronomical research. The observatory houses a remarkable collection of state-of-the-art telescopes operated by various international institutions.

Among its impressive array of instruments is the Gran Telescopio Canarias (GTC), the largest optical-infrared telescope in the world, which allows astronomers to peer deep into the universe and unravel its mysteries. The observatory is also home to the MAGIC (Major Atmospheric Gamma Imaging Cherenkov) telescopes, designed to study high-energy gamma rays emitted by celestial objects.

Visitors to the Roque de los Muchachos Observatory can participate in guided tours that provide a fascinating glimpse into the world of astronomical research. The tours include educational presentations about the observatory's telescopes, their scientific missions, and the groundbreaking discoveries made at this unique facility. Many tours also offer night-time stargazing sessions using professional-grade telescopes, allowing visitors to observe distant galaxies, nebulae, and star clusters under the guidance of expert astronomers.

Public and Amateur Observatories
La Palma also offers several public and amateur observatories where visitors can enjoy stargazing experiences without the need for specialized equipment or expertise.

Astro La Palma: Located in the town of Fuencaliente, Astro La Palma is a center dedicated to astrotourism and astronomy education. The center offers a variety of activities, including guided night-sky observations, astrophotography workshops, and telescope rentals. With its powerful telescopes and knowledgeable guides, Astro La Palma provides a fantastic opportunity for both novice and experienced stargazers to explore the wonders of the night sky.

Centro de Visitantes del Roque de Los Muchachos: This visitor center, located near the Roque de los Muchachos Observatory, features an interactive museum dedicated to astronomy and the natural environment of La Palma. The center offers guided night-sky tours that are perfect for families and amateur astronomers, providing a comprehensive introduction to the constellations, planets, and other celestial objects visible from La Palma.

Stargazing Spots

La Palma offers a multitude of excellent locations for stargazing, many of which are easily accessible and provide breathtaking views of the night sky.

Llano del Jable: This high-altitude plateau in the central part of the island offers expansive views of the night sky with minimal light pollution. Its remote location and elevated position make it a popular spot for amateur astronomers and astrophotographers.

Mirador del Time: Situated on the west coast near Tazacorte, this viewpoint offers stunning vistas of the Atlantic Ocean and clear night skies. It's an ideal spot for observing the Milky Way, a faint band of light stretching across the sky, composed of billions of stars.

Puntagorda Astronomical Viewpoint: This designated stargazing area in the village of Puntagorda is equipped with observation platforms and information panels, making it a great location for both novice and experienced stargazers. The viewpoint's design minimizes light pollution and provides clear views of the constellations and celestial objects.

El Paso: The area around the town of El Paso, including the Caldera de Taburiente National Park, provides excellent stargazing opportunities. The high altitude and clear skies make it a favorite spot for observing meteor showers, fleeting streaks of light caused by space debris entering the Earth's atmosphere, and deep-sky objects, such as galaxies and nebulae.

Astronomical Events and Festivals
La Palma hosts several astronomical events and festivals throughout the year, attracting astronomy enthusiasts from around the world and highlighting the island's commitment to astrotourism.

Transvulcania La Palma: This annual ultramarathon, held in May, includes night-time sections where participants can enjoy the island's spectacular starry skies while traversing challenging volcanic terrain. While primarily a sporting event, the Transvulcania La Palma showcases the island's unique combination of natural beauty and astronomical significance.

Starmus Festival: The Starmus Festival, a celebration of science, astronomy, and music, has also been held in the Canary Islands, including La Palma. This festival features lectures and workshops by renowned scientists and astronomers, as well as concerts and artistic performances inspired by the cosmos, creating a unique blend of scientific exploration and artistic expression.

Astrotourism Accommodation
Many accommodations on La Palma cater specifically to astrotourists, offering amenities and services that enhance the stargazing experience.

> **Hacienda de Abajo:** This luxury hotel in Tazacorte provides guided stargazing sessions and access to high-quality telescopes, allowing guests to explore the night sky in comfort and style.
>
> **La Palma & Teneguía Princess Vital & Fitness:** Located on the southwestern coast, this resort offers astronomy-themed activities, including night-sky tours and astrophotography workshops, catering to guests who wish to delve deeper into the wonders of the universe.
>
> **Ecofinca El Moral:** A rural retreat in the northern part of the island, Ecofinca El Moral provides a tranquil setting for stargazing, with minimal light pollution and access to telescopes, allowing guests to connect with nature and the cosmos.

Coastal Adventures
Watersports and Diving

Scuba Diving
La Palma's volcanic origins have created a fascinating underwater world, with unique geological formations and a rich biodiversity of marine life. The island offers a variety of dive sites that cater to all levels of experience, from beginners to seasoned divers.

> **Malpique:** Located near the southern tip of the island, Malpique is a dive site that combines history and natural beauty. The underwater memorial of stone crosses, placed to honor the martyrs of Tazacorte, adds a poignant touch to this unique dive site. The dramatic rock formations and abundant marine life, including schools of fish, octopuses, and the occasional barracuda, create a captivating underwater experience.

> **La Bombilla:** This dive site near Puerto Naos is known for its clear waters and fascinating underwater lava formations. Divers can explore tunnels and caverns, encountering a variety of marine species, such as moray eels, rays, and colorful nudibranchs, which are small, shell-less mollusks known for their vibrant colors and intricate patterns. La Bombilla offers both shallow and deeper dives, making it suitable for divers of all levels.

> **El Bajón:** Situated near the town of Los Llanos, El Bajón is a popular dive site characterized by its impressive volcanic rock formations. The site features a large underwater pinnacle that attracts a diverse range of marine life, including amberjacks, groupers, and the occasional shark, offering thrilling encounters for experienced divers.

The visibility at El Bajón is typically excellent, making it a favorite spot for underwater photographers.

Los Cancajos: This dive site near the capital, Santa Cruz de La Palma, provides a variety of diving experiences, from shallow reefs teeming with colorful fish to deeper drop-offs where pelagic species can be encountered. The underwater topography includes arches, tunnels, and rocky outcrops, providing endless opportunities for exploration and discovery.

Snorkeling
For those who prefer to stay closer to the surface, La Palma offers excellent snorkeling opportunities. The island's clear waters and diverse marine life make snorkeling a rewarding experience for all ages and abilities.

Charco Azul: Located in San Andrés y Sauces, Charco Azul is a series of natural seawater pools formed by volcanic rock. The calm, clear waters and sheltered environment make it an ideal spot for snorkeling, allowing visitors to observe a variety of fish and other marine creatures without venturing into the open ocean.

Playa de Los Cancajos: This black sand beach near Santa Cruz de La Palma is a popular spot for snorkeling, with its sheltered bay and clear waters providing excellent visibility. Snorkelers can encounter a variety of marine life, including octopuses, cuttlefish, and various species of colorful fish. The beach's convenient amenities, including sunbeds and showers, make it a comfortable and enjoyable place to spend a day snorkeling.

Puerto Naos: The waters around Puerto Naos offer excellent snorkeling opportunities, with a diverse range of marine life and interesting underwater rock formations to explore. The beach's calm waters and good visibility make it easy to observe the underwater world and discover hidden treasures.

Kayaking

Kayaking is a fantastic way to experience La Palma's dramatic coastline and explore its hidden coves, sea caves, and rugged cliffs. The island's calm waters and diverse marine environment make kayaking an enjoyable and rewarding activity.

> **Tijarafe Coast:** The coastline near Tijarafe is known for its dramatic cliffs, sea caves, and hidden beaches. Kayaking along this stretch of coast allows you to discover secluded coves, paddle through natural arches, and observe the island's volcanic formations from a unique perspective. The area is also home to a variety of marine life, including dolphins and seabirds, offering opportunities for wildlife encounters.

> **Tazacorte to Puerto Naos:** This kayaking route takes you along the west coast of La Palma, offering stunning views of the island's volcanic landscape and the vast expanse of the Atlantic Ocean. The calm waters and sheltered bays make it an ideal route for beginners, while more experienced kayakers can venture further out to explore the sea caves and rock formations along the coast.

Stand-Up Paddleboarding (SUP)

Stand-up paddleboarding (SUP) has become increasingly popular in La Palma, offering a unique way to experience the island's coastal beauty and enjoy a gentle workout. The calm waters and stunning scenery make SUP an ideal activity for all ages and abilities.

Playa de Puerto Naos: The calm waters and gentle waves of Playa de Puerto Naos make it a perfect spot for stand-up paddleboarding. The beach's expansive shoreline and clear waters provide ample space to paddle and explore the surrounding area.

Playa de Los Cancajos: This sheltered bay near Santa Cruz de La Palma is another great location for SUP. The calm waters and beautiful surroundings make it an ideal place to enjoy a leisurely paddle and observe the marine life that thrives in the bay.

Surfing and Bodyboarding

While La Palma may not be as renowned for surfing as some of the other Canary Islands, it still offers some excellent spots for surfing and bodyboarding. The island's volcanic coastline and consistent swells create challenging waves for experienced surfers and gentler waves for beginners.

Playa de Nogales: This beach, located on the northern coast, is considered one of the best surfing spots on La Palma. The powerful waves and consistent swells attract surfers from around the world, offering an exhilarating experience for those seeking a challenge.

Playa de Puerto Naos: The waves at Puerto Naos are more forgiving, making it a suitable spot for both beginners and experienced surfers. The beach offers a variety of breaks, catering to different skill levels and preferences.

Sailing

Sailing around La Palma offers a unique perspective of the island's coastline, allowing you to appreciate its dramatic cliffs, hidden coves, and diverse marine environment. The island's favorable winds and calm waters make it an ideal destination for sailing enthusiasts.

> **Santa Cruz de La Palma to Tazacorte:** This sailing route takes you along the eastern and southern coasts of La Palma, offering stunning views of the volcanic cliffs, lush forests, and charming coastal towns.

> **Los Llanos to Puerto Naos:** This route along the western coast provides a different perspective of the island's volcanic landscape, with opportunities to spot marine life such as dolphins and sea turtles.

Fishing

La Palma's rich marine environment offers excellent fishing opportunities for those seeking to cast a line and experience the thrill of the catch. The island's waters are home to a variety of fish species, from smaller reef fish to larger pelagic species.

> **Tazacorte:** This coastal town is a popular fishing destination, with its waters teeming with a variety of fish species, including tuna, marlin, and dorado. Several fishing charters operate from Tazacorte, offering guided fishing trips for both experienced anglers and beginners.

> **Fuencaliente:** The southern coast of La Palma, particularly around Fuencaliente, is known for its deep-sea fishing opportunities. Anglers can try their luck at catching large game fish such as tuna and marlin, experiencing the thrill of battling these powerful creatures in the deep blue waters.

Coastal Villages to Visit
- **Tazacorte**

Tazacorte, nestled on the western coast of La Palma, is one of the island's most picturesque and historically significant villages. As the oldest town in the Aridane Valley, Tazacorte boasts a rich history dating back to the Spanish conquest, with its charming streets and colorful houses reflecting its vibrant past.

The village is divided into two main areas: Tazacorte Pueblo and Puerto de Tazacorte. Tazacorte Pueblo, the old town, is a labyrinth of narrow streets lined with brightly painted houses, historic buildings, and a charming plaza where locals gather and time seems to slow down. The Church of San Miguel Arcángel, a 16th-century architectural gem, stands as a testament to the village's enduring faith and cultural heritage.

Puerto de Tazacorte, the harbor area, offers a contrasting yet complementary atmosphere. This bustling seaside district features a lively promenade lined with palm trees, inviting cafes, and restaurants serving fresh seafood delicacies. The harbor is a hub of activity, with fishing boats bobbing in the water and ferries departing for excursions to other Canary Islands. A beautiful black sand beach stretches along the coast, inviting visitors to relax, soak up the sun, and enjoy the refreshing waters of the Atlantic.

- **Puerto Naos**

Puerto Naos, located on the western coast of La Palma, is a vibrant village that has become a popular tourist destination, renowned for its beautiful black sand beach and lively atmosphere. The village's laid-back ambiance and range of amenities make it an ideal spot for a relaxing seaside getaway.

The main attraction in Puerto Naos is its expansive black sand beach, one of the most stunning on La Palma. The beach is backed by a palm-lined promenade that buzzes with activity, offering a variety of restaurants, bars, and shops where visitors can indulge in local cuisine, enjoy refreshing drinks, and find unique souvenirs. The area's subtropical climate ensures pleasant weather year-round, making it a perfect destination for sunbathing, swimming, and enjoying water sports.

Puerto Naos is also known for its excellent paragliding conditions, thanks to the favorable wind patterns along the coast. Visitors can soar above the village and the coastline, enjoying breathtaking aerial views of the island's diverse landscapes. Other water activities, such as snorkeling, diving, and paddleboarding, are also popular in Puerto Naos, allowing visitors to explore the underwater world and experience the island's natural beauty from a different perspective.

- **Santa Cruz de La Palma**

Santa Cruz de La Palma, the capital of La Palma, is a town steeped in history and cultural heritage. Located on the eastern coast, the town is renowned for its well-preserved colonial architecture, charming cobblestone streets, and picturesque plazas, offering a glimpse into the island's rich past.

The old town of Santa Cruz de La Palma is a treasure trove of historic buildings and landmarks, each with its own story to tell. The Plaza de España, the town's main square, is surrounded by beautiful Renaissance buildings, including the Town Hall and the Church of El Salvador, showcasing the architectural grandeur of the colonial era. The Real Castillo de Santa Catalina, a 16th-century fortress, stands guard over the harbor, offering panoramic views of the city and the sea, and serving as a reminder of the island's defensive history.

Visitors to Santa Cruz de La Palma can delve into the island's history and culture by exploring its many museums, including the Insular Museum, which houses a fascinating collection of artifacts and exhibits that tell the story of La Palma's evolution. The seaside promenade, Avenida Marítima, lined with traditional wooden balconies, offers a picturesque setting for leisurely strolls and enjoying the fresh sea breeze. Santa Cruz de La Palma also hosts numerous festivals and cultural events throughout the year, adding to its vibrant atmosphere and showcasing the island's traditions and artistic expressions.

- **Los Cancajos**

Los Cancajos, a coastal village located just a few kilometers south of Santa Cruz de La Palma, is a popular destination for its beautiful black sand beach and tranquil atmosphere. The village offers a range of accommodations, dining options, and recreational activities, making it an ideal base for exploring the island's eastern coast.

The main attraction in Los Cancajos is its beach, which is divided into two sections by a series of natural rock pools. These pools, formed by volcanic rock, offer a safe and calm swimming environment, perfect for families and those seeking a more relaxed beach experience. The clear waters and diverse marine life also make Los Cancajos an excellent spot for snorkeling and exploring the underwater world.

The village itself offers a variety of restaurants, bars, and shops, catering to a range of tastes and budgets. Visitors can enjoy traditional Canarian cuisine, international dishes, or simply relax with a refreshing drink while soaking in the coastal ambiance. Los Cancajos is also a popular starting point for exploring the nearby trails and natural parks, offering opportunities for hiking, birdwatching, and immersing oneself in the island's natural beauty.

Fuencaliente

Fuencaliente, located on the southern tip of La Palma, is a village that embodies the island's volcanic heritage and coastal beauty. The village is known for its dramatic landscapes, historic lighthouses, and salt flats, offering a unique blend of natural wonders and cultural attractions.

One of the main attractions in Fuencaliente is the Faro de Fuencaliente, a historic lighthouse complex that includes the old lighthouse, built in 1903, and the new lighthouse, built in 1985. The lighthouses stand as sentinels on the rugged coastline, offering panoramic views of the ocean and the surrounding volcanic landscapes. The nearby Salinas de Fuencaliente, a series of salt flats where seawater is evaporated to produce sea salt, is another popular attraction. The salt flats are not only a site of natural beauty but also an important habitat for migratory birds, attracting birdwatchers and nature enthusiasts.

Visitors to Fuencaliente can explore the volcanic landscapes created by the eruptions of the San Antonio and Teneguía volcanoes, the youngest volcanoes on the island. The hiking trails in the area offer stunning views of the volcanic craters, lava flows, and the dramatic coastline. The beaches near Fuencaliente, such as Playa de Echentive, provide excellent opportunities for swimming, snorkeling, and sunbathing, with their black volcanic sand and clear waters.

Puntagorda

Puntagorda, a charming village on the northwestern coast of La Palma, is known for its agricultural heritage, scenic landscapes, and peaceful atmosphere. The village is surrounded by lush orchards and terraced fields, where a variety of fruits and vegetables are cultivated, showcasing the island's fertile volcanic soil and agricultural traditions.

The Mirador de Miraflores, a viewpoint near Puntagorda, offers breathtaking panoramic views of the coastline, the vast expanse of the Atlantic Ocean, and the neighboring island of Tenerife. The village's historic center features traditional Canarian architecture, with whitewashed houses, cobblestone streets, and a beautiful church, the Iglesia de San Mauro Abad.

Puntagorda is an ideal destination for those seeking tranquility and a connection with nature. The nearby Barranco de las Angustias gorge offers stunning hiking trails that lead through lush vegetation and along dramatic cliffs, providing a challenging but rewarding experience for outdoor enthusiasts. The village's farmers' market, held every weekend, is a vibrant hub of activity, where visitors can sample local produce, crafts, and culinary delights, experiencing the authentic flavors and traditions of La Palma.

Garafía
Garafía, a remote and picturesque village on the northern coast of La Palma, offers a glimpse into the island's rural heritage and its connection to the cosmos. The village is characterized by its rugged landscapes, dramatic cliffs, deep ravines, and lush greenery, providing a haven for nature lovers and those seeking tranquility.

One of the main attractions in Garafía is the Roque de los Muchachos, the highest point on the island and home to the world-renowned Roque de los Muchachos Observatory. The observatory, with its impressive collection of telescopes, attracts scientists and researchers from around the globe, studying the mysteries of the universe. Visitors can enjoy guided tours of the observatory and participate in night-sky observations, marveling at the clarity and brilliance of the stars under La Palma's pristine skies.

The village of Garafía itself exudes a traditional charm, with its historic center featuring traditional Canarian houses, a beautiful church, and narrow streets that invite exploration. The coastline near Garafía is dotted with hidden coves and natural pools, offering stunning views of the Atlantic Ocean and opportunities for swimming and relaxation.

Garafía is a paradise for hikers and outdoor enthusiasts, with a variety of trails that lead through lush forests, along dramatic cliffs, and to remote beaches. The village's commitment to preserving its dark skies and promoting astrotourism makes it a unique and unforgettable destination for those seeking to connect with the wonders of the universe.

Boat Tours and Excursions
Dolphin and Whale Watching Tours

The waters surrounding La Palma are teeming with marine life, making it a prime destination for dolphin and whale watching. Several tour operators offer excursions that provide unforgettable encounters with these majestic creatures in their natural habitat.

>**Los Llanos de Aridane:** The deep waters off the coast of Los Llanos de Aridane, particularly near Puerto de Tazacorte, provide ideal conditions for spotting dolphins, pilot whales, and even the occasional sperm whale. Experienced guides accompany these tours, providing fascinating insights into the different species, their behaviors, and the importance of marine conservation.

>**Santa Cruz de La Palma:** The capital city also offers dolphin and whale watching tours, departing from the harbor and venturing into the Atlantic Ocean in search of these magnificent creatures. Some tours include additional activities, such as snorkeling stops, allowing you to

explore the underwater world and encounter a variety of marine life.

Coastal Exploration Tours
La Palma's coastline is a masterpiece of nature, with rugged cliffs, hidden coves, and volcanic formations that create a dramatic and captivating landscape. Coastal exploration tours provide a unique perspective on the island's geology and natural beauty.

> **Roques de la Bajada:** This tour takes you along the western coast of La Palma, where you'll witness the impressive Roques de la Bajada, a series of striking sea stacks and volcanic outcrops that rise majestically from the ocean. The tour typically includes stops at secluded beaches, offering opportunities for swimming, snorkeling, and exploring the island's hidden coastal gems.
>
> **Fuencaliente:** The southern coast of La Palma, around Fuencaliente, is renowned for its volcanic landscapes, formed by past eruptions and lava flows. Coastal tours in this area often include visits to the historic Fuencaliente Lighthouse, a landmark that has guided sailors for centuries, and the nearby salt flats, where traditional methods are used to harvest sea salt. The contrast between the black volcanic rock and the azure waters creates a mesmerizing and unforgettable experience.

Sunset and Evening Cruises
For a more relaxed and romantic experience, consider a sunset or evening cruise along La Palma's coastline. These tours provide the perfect opportunity to unwind, enjoy the tranquility of the sea, and witness the beauty of the island as the sun dips below the horizon.

Puerto Naos: Sunset cruises departing from Puerto Naos are a popular choice, offering stunning views of the western coastline as the sun paints the sky with vibrant colors. These tours often include a glass of champagne or local wine, allowing you to toast to the breathtaking scenery and create a memorable experience.

Tazacorte: Evening cruises from Tazacorte offer a similar experience, with the added charm of departing from the village's picturesque harbor. Some tours may also include live music or a traditional Canarian dinner, enhancing the romantic ambiance and providing a taste of the island's culinary delights.

Fishing Charters

La Palma's rich marine environment makes it a fantastic destination for fishing enthusiasts. Fishing charters offer the chance to experience the thrill of the catch, with opportunities to reel in a variety of species, from smaller coastal fish to larger game fish that inhabit the deeper waters.

Tazacorte: Several charter companies operate from Tazacorte, offering both half-day and full-day fishing trips that cater to all levels of experience. These charters provide all the necessary equipment and guidance, making them suitable for both seasoned anglers and those new to fishing. Common catches in the waters around Tazacorte include tuna, marlin, and dorado, offering an exciting challenge for fishing enthusiasts.

Santa Cruz de La Palma: Fishing charters also depart from Santa Cruz de La Palma, providing access to the island's eastern waters and a different perspective on the marine environment. These trips often include the opportunity to learn about local fishing techniques and traditions from experienced local fishermen.

Sailing Adventures

Sailing excursions around La Palma offer a serene and scenic way to explore the island's coastline and enjoy the freedom of the open water. Whether you're an experienced sailor or a novice, sailing tours provide a unique perspective on La Palma's natural beauty.

> **Los Cancajos:** Sailing tours from Los Cancajos typically include a mix of coastal exploration and open-water sailing, allowing you to discover hidden coves, admire the dramatic cliffs, and enjoy the refreshing sea breeze. The clear waters and favorable winds make for an enjoyable experience, regardless of your sailing expertise.

> **Puerto Naos:** Sailing adventures departing from Puerto Naos offer similar experiences, with the chance to explore the island's western coast and its diverse marine life. These tours often include stops at secluded coves and beaches, where you can swim, snorkel, or simply relax on the shore, enjoying the tranquility of La Palma's coastal paradise.

Catamaran Tours

Catamaran tours are a popular option for exploring La Palma's coastline in comfort and style. These spacious vessels offer a stable and comfortable ride, making them ideal for families, larger groups, and those seeking a more relaxed experience on the water.

> **Tazacorte:** Catamaran tours from Tazacorte offer a range of experiences, from half-day trips to full-day excursions that explore the island's western coastline. These tours often include amenities such as onboard barbecues, where

you can enjoy freshly grilled seafood, snorkel gear for exploring the underwater world, and spacious sunbathing decks for soaking up the sun and enjoying the panoramic views.

Santa Cruz de La Palma: Catamaran tours from Santa Cruz de La Palma offer similar experiences, with the added charm of exploring the island's eastern shores and its unique coastal formations. These tours provide an excellent way to observe the island's dramatic cliffs, hidden coves, and diverse marine life, all while enjoying the comfort and stability of a catamaran.

Island Hopping Excursions

La Palma's location within the Canary Islands archipelago makes it an excellent base for island hopping excursions. These tours allow you to venture beyond La Palma and discover the unique charm and beauty of neighboring islands.

La Gomera: Island hopping tours to La Gomera typically include visits to the island's lush laurel forests, known as "laurisilva," which are a UNESCO World Heritage Site. These ancient forests, with their unique flora and fauna, offer a fascinating glimpse into a prehistoric ecosystem. The tours may also include visits to charming villages, dramatic cliffs, and opportunities for hiking and exploring the island's natural wonders.

El Hierro: El Hierro, the smallest of the Canary Islands, is a haven for nature lovers and adventure seekers. Island hopping tours to El Hierro offer the chance to explore its rugged volcanic landscapes, pristine waters, and unique cultural heritage.

Tenerife: Tenerife, the largest of the Canary Islands, offers a diverse range of attractions, from the majestic Mount Teide, Spain's highest peak, to the vibrant cities of Santa Cruz de Tenerife and La Laguna. Island hopping tours to Tenerife often focus on the island's natural and cultural highlights, providing a taste of its diverse offerings.

Glass-Bottom Boat Tours

Glass-bottom boat tours provide a unique and accessible way to explore La Palma's underwater world without getting wet. These tours offer an up-close view of the island's marine life and underwater landscapes, making them ideal for families, those who are not comfortable swimming, or anyone who wants to experience the beauty of the ocean from a different perspective.

Puerto Naos: Glass-bottom boat tours from Puerto Naos typically explore the island's western coast, offering excellent views of the volcanic rock formations, colorful fish, and other marine creatures that inhabit these waters.

Los Cancajos: Glass-bottom boat tours from Los Cancajos offer similar experiences, with the added bonus of exploring the island's eastern shores and its unique underwater ecosystems.

Culinary Delights
Traditional Canarian Cuisine

- **Papas Arrugadas**

Papas Arrugadas, or wrinkled potatoes, are a quintessential Canarian dish and a must-try for any visitor to La Palma. These small potatoes are cooked in heavily salted water until their skins become wrinkled and a light salt crust forms on the outside. The potatoes are typically served with mojo sauce, a staple condiment in Canarian cuisine that adds a burst of flavor to the dish.

Mojo comes in two main varieties: mojo verde (green sauce) and mojo rojo (red sauce). Mojo verde is made with a blend of cilantro, green peppers, garlic, olive oil, and vinegar, creating a vibrant and herbaceous sauce. Mojo rojo, on the other hand, is made with red peppers, paprika, garlic, olive oil, and vinegar, offering a tangy and slightly spicy flavor. The combination of the salty potatoes and the flavorful mojo sauces creates a delightful harmony of textures and tastes, making this dish a beloved staple in Canarian cuisine.

- **Gofio**

Gofio, a type of flour made from toasted grains, is a cornerstone of Canarian cuisine and a reflection of the island's agricultural heritage. Traditionally made from maize or wheat, gofio has a nutty, slightly sweet flavor and is packed with nutrients. This versatile ingredient can be used in a variety of dishes, both sweet and savory, showcasing the ingenuity and resourcefulness of Canarian cooking.

Gofio is often mixed with water or milk to create a dough-like consistency, which can be served as a side dish or used as a base for other preparations. It can also be added to soups and stews as a thickening agent, providing a hearty and nutritious element to these dishes. For a sweet treat, gofio can be combined with honey and nuts to make a dessert called gofio amasado, a simple yet satisfying indulgence.

- **Sancocho Canario**

Sancocho Canario is a beloved fish stew that is enjoyed throughout the Canary Islands, including La Palma. This traditional dish typically features salted fish, such as sea bass or grouper, which is boiled and served with papas arrugadas and mojo sauce. The fish is often accompanied by a variety of vegetables, such as sweet potatoes, carrots, and onions, adding sweetness and texture to the dish.

Sancocho Canario is a hearty and flavorful stew that showcases the island's abundant seafood and traditional cooking methods. The combination of the tender fish, flavorful vegetables, and tangy mojo sauce creates a satisfying and authentic Canarian culinary experience.

- **Rancho Canario**

Rancho Canario is a traditional Canarian stew that is perfect for cooler days or when you're craving a comforting and flavorful meal. This hearty stew is made with a variety of meats, such as beef, pork, or chicken, along with chickpeas, potatoes, and noodles. The stew is simmered in a rich broth made from vegetables, tomatoes, and spices, creating a symphony of flavors that meld together beautifully.

Rancho Canario is a reflection of the island's agricultural heritage, combining locally sourced meats and vegetables with simple yet flavorful ingredients. This dish is a staple in Canarian households and a testament to the island's culinary traditions.

- **Queso Asado**

Queso Asado, or grilled cheese, is a popular dish in La Palma that showcases the island's cheese-making traditions. The cheese, often made from goat's milk, is grilled until it develops a crispy, golden-brown crust, adding a delightful texture to the dish. The grilled cheese is then drizzled with mojo sauce or honey, creating a contrast of flavors that tantalize the taste buds.

The combination of the crispy exterior and the soft, melty interior of the cheese, combined with the tangy mojo sauce or sweet honey, makes Queso Asado a delightful appetizer or snack. It's a simple yet satisfying dish that highlights the quality of local ingredients and the culinary creativity of La Palma.

- **Carne de Cabra**

Carne de Cabra, or goat meat, is a traditional ingredient in Canarian cuisine, particularly in rural areas where goat herding has been a way of life for centuries. The meat is typically marinated with a mixture of garlic, thyme, bay leaves, and wine, allowing the flavors to penetrate the meat and tenderize it. It is then slow-cooked until it is incredibly tender and flavorful.

Carne de Cabra is often served with potatoes or gofio, creating a hearty and satisfying meal that reflects the island's pastoral traditions. The rich, flavorful meat is a must-try for those seeking an authentic taste of La Palma's culinary heritage.

- **Bienmesabe**

Bienmesabe, a traditional Canarian dessert, is as delightful as its name suggests. The name "bienmesabe" translates to "tastes good to me," and it is a fitting description for this sweet and indulgent treat. Bienmesabe is made from a blend of almonds, sugar, egg yolks, lemon zest, and cinnamon, cooked to a thick, creamy consistency that melts in your mouth.

This rich and flavorful dessert is often served with ice cream or pastries, adding a touch of sweetness and indulgence to any meal. Bienmesabe is a popular treat during festivals and celebrations, representing the celebratory spirit of La Palma's culture.

- **Ropa Vieja**

Ropa Vieja, meaning "old clothes" in Spanish, is a traditional Canarian dish that is also popular in other parts of the Spanish-speaking world. The name refers to the dish's origins as a way to use up leftover meat and vegetables, transforming them into a flavorful and comforting stew.

Ropa Vieja typically features shredded beef or chicken, chickpeas, potatoes, and a variety of vegetables, all cooked in a rich tomato-based sauce. The combination of textures and flavors creates a satisfying and hearty meal that is a staple in Canarian households.

Must-Try Dishes and Restaurants
Must-Try Dishes

Embark on a culinary exploration of La Palma with these must-try dishes that showcase the island's unique flavors and culinary traditions.

Papas Arrugadas (Wrinkled Potatoes): Papas Arrugadas are arguably the most famous dish in Canarian cuisine, a staple that embodies the island's culinary identity. These small potatoes are boiled in heavily salted water until their skins become wrinkled and a light salt crust forms on the outside. The potatoes are typically served with mojo sauce, a flavorful condiment that adds a tangy and spicy kick to the dish. Mojo comes in two main varieties: mojo verde (green sauce), made with cilantro and green peppers, and mojo rojo (red sauce), made with red peppers and paprika. The combination of the salty potatoes and the vibrant mojo sauces creates a symphony of flavors that is both simple and unforgettable.

Sancocho Canario: Sancocho Canario is a traditional fish stew that is a must-try when visiting La Palma. This hearty and flavorful dish features salted fish, usually sea bass or grouper, which is boiled and served with papas arrugadas and mojo sauce. The fish is often accompanied by a variety of vegetables, such as sweet potatoes, carrots, and onions, adding sweetness and texture to the stew. Sancocho Canario is a true representation of the island's culinary heritage, showcasing the abundance of fresh seafood and the traditional cooking methods that have been passed down through generations.

Rancho Canario: Rancho Canario is a traditional Canarian stew that embodies the island's agricultural heritage. This hearty and comforting dish is made with a variety of meats, such as beef, pork, or chicken, along with chickpeas, potatoes, and noodles. The stew is simmered in a rich broth made from tomatoes, vegetables, and spices, creating a symphony of flavors that meld together beautifully. Rancho Canario is a satisfying and flavorful meal that reflects the island's connection to its land and its culinary traditions.

Queso Asado (Grilled Cheese): Queso Asado is a popular appetizer in La Palma that showcases the island's cheese-making traditions. This simple yet delicious dish features grilled cheese, usually made from goat's milk, which is grilled until it develops a crispy, golden-brown crust. The grilled cheese is then drizzled with mojo sauce or honey, creating a delightful contrast of flavors and textures. The combination of the crispy exterior and the soft, melty interior of the cheese, along with the tangy sauce or sweet honey, makes Queso Asado a delightful treat for the taste buds.

Carne de Cabra (Goat Meat): Carne de Cabra, or goat meat, is a traditional ingredient in Canarian cuisine, particularly in rural areas where goat herding has been a way of life for centuries. The meat is typically marinated with a mixture of garlic, thyme, bay leaves, and wine, allowing the flavors to penetrate the meat and tenderize it. It is then slow-cooked until it is incredibly tender and flavorful, often served with potatoes or gofio as accompaniments. Carne de Cabra is a rich and flavorful dish that reflects the island's pastoral traditions and is a must-try for meat lovers seeking an authentic taste of La Palma.

Bienmesabe: Bienmesabe, meaning "tastes good to me" in Spanish, is a traditional Canarian dessert that lives up to its name. This sweet and indulgent treat is made from a blend of almonds, sugar, egg yolks, lemon zest, and cinnamon, cooked to a thick, creamy consistency that is both rich and flavorful. Bienmesabe is often served with ice cream or pastries, adding a touch of sweetness and decadence to any meal.

Almogrote: Almogrote is a traditional Canarian spread made from aged cheese, garlic, peppers, and olive oil. This flavorful spread has a thick, paste-like consistency and is typically served as a dip for bread or crackers. The flavor of almogrote is rich and savory, with a hint of spiciness from the peppers, making it a delicious appetizer or snack that showcases the robust flavors of Canarian cheese.

Potaje de Berros (Watercress Soup): Potaje de Berros is a traditional Canarian soup that is both nutritious and flavorful. This hearty soup is made with watercress, a leafy green vegetable that is abundant on the island, along with potatoes, corn, and other vegetables. The soup is flavored with garlic, onions, and sometimes bacon or chorizo, adding depth and complexity to its taste. Potaje de Berros is a satisfying and wholesome dish that is often enjoyed as a main course, especially during the cooler months.

Pollo al Salmorejo (Chicken in Salmorejo Sauce): Pollo al Salmorejo is a flavorful chicken dish that features tender chicken marinated in a rich and tangy salmorejo sauce. The sauce is typically made with a blend of garlic, paprika, cumin, vinegar, and olive oil, creating a complex and aromatic marinade that infuses the chicken with flavor. The chicken is then baked or grilled until it is cooked through and slightly crispy on the outside, while remaining juicy and tender on the inside. Pollo al Salmorejo is a popular dish for family gatherings and special occasions, showcasing the culinary creativity and flavorful traditions of La Palma.

Top Restaurants

Here are some of the top restaurants to explore on your culinary journey through La Palma:

Restaurante Chipi-Chipi (Santa Cruz de La Palma): This beloved local eatery is known for its authentic Canarian dishes and warm, welcoming atmosphere. Restaurante Chipi-Chipi is a favorite among locals and visitors alike, offering a taste of traditional La Palma cuisine in a relaxed and friendly setting. Their papas arrugadas and mojo sauce are a must-try, as are their grilled meats and fresh seafood dishes.

El Duende del Fuego (Los Llanos de Aridane): El Duende del Fuego offers a cozy and inviting ambiance, with a menu that highlights local ingredients and traditional flavors with a creative twist. The restaurant is known for its delicious gofio amasado, a traditional Canarian dessert, as well as its innovative interpretations of classic dishes like sancocho canario.

Bodegón Tamanca (Fuencaliente): Nestled in the heart of the wine-producing region of Fuencaliente, Bodegón Tamanca is a rustic restaurant housed in a traditional Canarian bodega. The restaurant specializes in grilled meats, including carne de cabra (goat meat), a local delicacy, and offers a selection of local wines to complement the hearty cuisine. The cozy, cave-like interior and friendly service create a memorable dining experience.

Casa Goyo (Breña Baja): Casa Goyo is a popular restaurant known for its fresh seafood and traditional Canarian dishes. Situated near the coast, the restaurant offers beautiful views of the ocean, providing a scenic backdrop for enjoying a delicious meal. The menu features a variety of fish dishes, including sancocho canario, as well as classic Canarian accompaniments like papas arrugadas and mojo sauce.

Restaurante Balcón Taburiente (Caldera de Taburiente National Park): Perched on the edge of the Caldera de Taburiente, this restaurant offers breathtaking views of the national park's dramatic landscapes. The menu features local ingredients and traditional recipes, with highlights including queso asado (grilled cheese) and potaje de berros (watercress soup). Restaurante Balcón Taburiente is a must-visit for those exploring the national park, offering a unique dining experience amidst stunning natural beauty.

La Casa del Volcán (Fuencaliente): Located near the Teneguía volcano in Fuencaliente, La Casa del Volcán provides a unique dining experience with a focus on local cuisine and volcanic landscapes. The restaurant's menu features traditional Canarian dishes such as conejo en salmorejo (rabbit in salmorejo sauce) and rancho canario, as well as a selection of local wines that reflect the island's terroir.

El Jardín de la Sal (Fuencaliente): Situated near the Fuencaliente salt flats, El Jardín de la Sal offers fresh seafood and stunning ocean views. The restaurant's menu features a variety of fish dishes, including churros de pescado (fish churros) and sancocho canario, as well as traditional Canarian accompaniments like papas arrugadas and mojo sauce. The outdoor terrace provides a picturesque setting for enjoying a meal while taking in the beauty of the salt flats and the surrounding coastline.

Restaurante El Encuentro (Santa Cruz de La Palma): Restaurante El Encuentro offers a blend of traditional and modern Canarian cuisine, showcasing the island's culinary heritage with a contemporary twist. The menu features dishes such as pollo al salmorejo (chicken in salmorejo sauce), almogrote (a traditional cheese spread), and ropa vieja (a flavorful stew), as well as a variety of vegetarian options. The stylish interior and attentive service make it a popular choice for a special dining experience.

Mesón del Mar (Puerto Naos): Located in the coastal village of Puerto Naos, Mesón del Mar is a seafood restaurant known for its fresh catches and traditional Canarian dishes. The menu features a variety of fish and shellfish, including grilled octopus, prawns, and sancocho canario. The restaurant's beachfront location and relaxed atmosphere make it a great spot for a casual meal by the sea.

Local Markets and Food Festivals
Local Markets
Mercado Municipal de Santa Cruz de La Palma: Located in the heart of the capital city, the Mercado Municipal de Santa Cruz de La Palma is a bustling hub of activity, where locals and visitors alike gather to purchase fresh ingredients and experience the island's culinary delights. Open from early morning until early afternoon, the market offers a wide range of fresh produce, including locally grown fruits and vegetables, a variety of meats and cheeses, and an impressive selection of seafood caught in the surrounding waters. The Mercado Municipal is a feast for the senses, with colorful displays, enticing aromas, and the lively chatter of vendors and shoppers.

Mercadillo del Agricultor de Puntagorda: Nestled in the picturesque village of Puntagorda, the Mercadillo del Agricultor is one of the most popular markets on the island. This vibrant market, open on weekends, offers a unique opportunity to connect with local farmers and artisans. Vendors showcase their organic and seasonal produce, including a variety of fruits, vegetables, and fresh juices. The market also features stalls selling local wines, plants, flowers, handicrafts, and homemade preserves, providing a taste of La Palma's agricultural bounty and creative spirit. The market's location amidst beautiful pine forests adds to its charm, creating a relaxed and scenic atmosphere for shoppers.

Mercadillo Municipal de Puntallana: The Mercadillo Municipal de Puntallana, held in the charming village of Puntallana, is another delightful market that showcases the island's local products. Open on weekends, the market offers a variety of fresh produce, cheeses, meats, and artisanal goods, all sourced from the surrounding region. The market's scenic location and friendly atmosphere make it a pleasant place to browse, sample local delicacies, and discover unique souvenirs.

Mercadillo de Breña Alta: The Mercadillo de Breña Alta is a vibrant market held in the town of Breña Alta, offering a wide selection of fresh fruits, vegetables, meats, cheeses, and seafood. This bustling market is a great place to find high-quality local products, interact with friendly vendors, and experience the lively atmosphere of a traditional Canarian market.

Mercadillo de Mazo: Located in the town of Mazo, the Mercadillo de Mazo is known for its fresh produce and artisanal goods. The market offers a variety of fruits, vegetables, meats, cheeses, and handmade crafts, showcasing the island's agricultural and artistic traditions. It's a wonderful place to immerse yourself in the local culture, discover unique souvenirs, and taste the flavors of La Palma.

Food Festivals

La Palma's food festivals are a celebration of the island's culinary heritage, showcasing its diverse flavors, traditional dishes, and the passion of its people for food and community.

Gastronomic Festival Saborea La Palma: The Gastronomic Festival Saborea La Palma is a highlight of the island's culinary calendar, held annually in November. This festival is a true celebration of La Palma's gastronomy, with a variety of food stalls, cooking demonstrations, and tastings that showcase the island's diverse culinary offerings. Visitors can indulge in a wide range of local dishes, from the iconic papas arrugadas and mojo sauces to traditional Canarian desserts and local wines. The festival is a feast for the senses, with enticing aromas, vibrant colors, and a lively atmosphere that celebrates the island's culinary traditions.

Los Indianos Festival: The Los Indianos Festival, celebrated on Carnival Monday in Santa Cruz de La Palma, is a unique and colorful event that commemorates the return of La Palma's emigrants from Latin America, particularly Cuba. Participants dress in all-white attire, reminiscent of the colonial era, and engage in a playful battle of talcum powder, creating a cloud of white that fills the streets and adds to the festive atmosphere. The festival is a joyous celebration of the island's cultural heritage and its connection to its diaspora, with music, dance, and a lively atmosphere that invites everyone to join in the fun.

Fiesta de San Antonio del Monte: The Fiesta de San Antonio del Monte, held in Garafía in June, is a traditional festival that blends religion, livestock, music, and local food. This unique celebration showcases the island's rural traditions and its connection to agriculture and livestock farming. Visitors can enjoy animal exhibitions, competitions, and a variety of local dishes, experiencing the authentic flavors and customs of La Palma's rural communities.

Fiesta del Almendro: The Fiesta del Almendro, celebrated in Puntagorda at the end of January, is a delightful festival that marks the blossoming of the almond trees, a symbol of spring and renewal. The festival features music, dances, and a variety of sweets and treats made with almonds, showcasing the island's natural beauty and culinary creativity.

Corpus Christi in Villa de Mazo: The Corpus Christi festival in Villa de Mazo is a grand celebration that transforms the town's streets into a visual feast. The festival features elaborate arches and carpets made from natural ingredients such as flowers, plants, and moss, creating intricate patterns and religious scenes. The Corpus Christi festival is a testament to the island's artistic talent and religious devotion, offering a glimpse into its cultural heritage and community spirit.

La Palma Blue Experience: The La Palma Blue Experience is a music festival held in December that celebrates the island's natural beauty and musical talent. This unique festival features performances by local and international artists, set against the stunning backdrop of La Palma's landscapes. The La Palma Blue Experience offers a harmonious blend of music and nature, providing a memorable experience for music lovers and those seeking to connect with the island's creative spirit.

Craft Fair in Santa Cruz de La Palma: The Craft Fair in Santa Cruz de La Palma is a popular event held in November that showcases the island's rich tradition of craftsmanship. The fair features a variety of handmade crafts, including pottery, jewelry, textiles, and woodwork, all created by local artisans. Visitors can browse through the stalls, admire the intricate designs, and purchase unique souvenirs that reflect the island's cultural heritage.

Wine and Craft Beer Tasting
The Charm of La Palma's Wineries
La Palma's winemaking tradition dates back to the 16th century, when Spanish settlers recognized the potential of the island's volcanic soil and unique climate for cultivating grapes. The island's vineyards, often perched on steep slopes and terraced hillsides, produce wines with distinctive character and a deep connection to the land.

El Paso and Tijarafe: Vineyards in the Clouds: In the higher altitudes of El Paso and Tijarafe, vineyards are often shrouded in mist, creating an ethereal atmosphere and lending a mystical quality to the winemaking process. The cooler temperatures and volcanic soil in these regions produce wines with unique characteristics, particularly the whites made from the indigenous Albillo Criollo grape. These wines are known for their aromatic complexity, with notes of citrus fruits, floral hints, and a subtle minerality, complemented by a refreshing acidity that makes them a perfect pairing for local seafood and cheeses. Visiting these vineyards offers not only a tasting experience but also breathtaking views of the island's rugged terrain, where the vines seem to cling to the slopes, reaching for the sky.

Fuencaliente: The Heart of Malvasia: Fuencaliente, located in the south of La Palma, is renowned for its Malvasia wines. The volcanic soil, combined with the sunny and arid climate of this region, creates ideal conditions for cultivating the Malvasia grape, a variety that has been grown on the island for centuries. The Malvasia grape produces both dry and sweet wines, each with its own distinct character. The dry Malvasia wines are known for their aromatic complexity and refreshing acidity, while the sweet Malvasia wines are a true indulgence, with notes of honey, dried fruits, and a hint of volcanic minerality. The region's wineries often provide guided tours, offering visitors a chance to learn about the winemaking process, from grape cultivation and harvesting to fermentation, aging, and bottling. These tours often include tastings, where you can savor the unique flavors of La Palma's Malvasia wines while enjoying panoramic views of the Atlantic Ocean.

Puntagorda and Garafía: Hidden Gems: For those seeking a more intimate and authentic wine experience, the regions of Puntagorda and Garafía offer a rustic charm and a glimpse into the island's traditional winemaking practices. Here, small family-owned wineries, often passed down through generations, produce limited-production wines that reflect a deep connection to the land and the island's heritage. The wines, often crafted from Listán Blanco and Listán Negro grapes, two of the most widely planted varieties in the Canary Islands, exhibit a unique character, with flavors that reflect the volcanic soil, the Atlantic breezes, and the passion of the winemakers. Tasting sessions at these wineries are often intimate affairs, with the winemakers themselves sharing stories of their families, their vineyards, and the traditions that have shaped their craft.

La Palma's Craft Beer Scene

While La Palma's winemaking heritage is well-established, its craft beer scene is a relatively recent addition to the island's culinary landscape. However, it has quickly gained momentum, with innovative breweries popping up across the island, each offering unique and flavorful brews that reflect La Palma's distinct terroir and the creativity of its brewers.

Cervecería Isla Verde: Pioneers of La Palma's Craft Beer: Cervecería Isla Verde, located in Tijarafe, is a pioneer in La Palma's craft beer movement. Founded with a commitment to quality, innovation, and sustainability, this brewery has been instrumental in introducing craft beer culture to the island. Isla Verde offers a range of beers that cater to diverse palates, from refreshing lagers and pale ales to hoppy IPAs and rich stouts. Their "Garimba" series is particularly noteworthy, featuring beers brewed with local fruits and spices, such as bananas, oranges, and gofio, creating unique flavor profiles that capture the essence of La Palma. A visit to Isla Verde provides an opportunity to sample their diverse offerings, learn about the brewing process, and experience the passion and creativity that goes into each beer. The brewery often hosts events and tastings, creating a lively atmosphere where beer enthusiasts can gather and celebrate the island's burgeoning craft beer scene.

Craft Beer Festivals: A Celebration of Flavors: Throughout the year, La Palma hosts several craft beer festivals that bring together local breweries and beer lovers from across the island. These festivals are a fantastic opportunity to explore the island's evolving beer culture, with numerous stalls offering a wide variety of brews, from traditional styles to innovative creations. The festivals often feature live music, food trucks serving delicious local cuisine, and a vibrant atmosphere that celebrates the camaraderie and creativity of the craft beer community.

Pairing Experiences
No tasting experience in La Palma would be complete without pairing the island's exceptional wines and craft beers with its delectable cuisine. Many wineries and breweries collaborate with

local chefs to offer tasting menus that showcase the synergy between food and drink, creating a harmonious culinary experience.

Imagine savoring a glass of Malvasia, with its notes of honey and dried fruits, alongside a plate of grilled seafood, the wine's acidity cutting through the richness of the fish. Or perhaps enjoying a crisp, refreshing craft beer, brewed with local ingredients, alongside a platter of locally sourced cheeses and charcuterie, the beer's hop bitterness balancing the creamy textures and salty flavors. These pairing experiences not only enhance the individual flavors of the food and drink but also create a symphony of taste that reflects the island's gastronomic heritage.

Exploring Beyond the Glass
Wine and craft beer tasting in La Palma is more than just a culinary experience; it's an opportunity to immerse yourself in the island's culture, history, and natural beauty. Many tasting tours include visits to historic sites, walks through vineyards and orchards, and interactions with the passionate individuals who dedicate their lives to their craft.

As you sip on a glass of exquisite wine, produced from grapes grown on volcanic slopes, or savor a meticulously brewed craft beer, infused with local ingredients, you are not only indulging in a sensory delight but also partaking in a tradition that celebrates the essence of La Palma. You'll learn about the island's history, its unique terroir, and the dedication of the people who create these exceptional beverages.

Cultural and Art Experiences
Local Art and Craftsmanship

The Art of Embroidery
Embroidery in La Palma is more than just a decorative craft; it's a living tradition that has been passed down through generations, carrying with it stories, emotions, and a deep connection to the island's cultural heritage. The island's embroiderers, known as "bordadoras," are highly skilled artisans who meticulously create intricate designs and patterns using needle and thread.

> **Traditional Motifs and Techniques:** The embroidery of La Palma often features traditional motifs inspired by the island's natural beauty, including floral patterns, geometric shapes, and representations of local flora and fauna. The bordadoras employ a variety of stitches and techniques, passed down through generations, to create intricate and delicate designs that adorn traditional Canarian costumes, household linens, and religious vestments.

> **Breña Alta and Breña Baja: Hubs of Embroidery:** The municipalities of Breña Alta and Breña Baja are renowned for their embroidery workshops, where visitors can witness the bordadoras at work, their nimble fingers weaving intricate patterns with remarkable precision and artistry. These workshops offer a glimpse into the dedication and skill required to create these exquisite pieces, providing a deeper appreciation for the island's embroidery tradition.

> **La Palma Lace: A Delicate Tradition:** La Palma is also known for its delicate lacework, known as "encaje." This intricate craft requires a high level of dexterity and

precision, with artisans using fine threads to create airy and intricate patterns. La Palma lace is often incorporated into clothing, accessories, and decorative items, adding a touch of elegance and sophistication.

Pottery

Pottery is one of the oldest crafts on La Palma, with roots tracing back to the island's indigenous Benahoaritas. The tradition has evolved over centuries, blending pre-Hispanic techniques with Spanish influences to create a distinctive style that reflects the island's unique cultural identity.

Barlovento: The Cradle of Traditional Pottery: Barlovento, located in the northern part of the island, is a key center for traditional pottery. Here, artisans use locally sourced clay to create a variety of functional and decorative items, from everyday household utensils to artistic pieces that adorn homes and gardens. The process of creating pottery in Barlovento involves several stages, including the collection and preparation of the clay, shaping the clay into the desired forms, drying the pieces, and firing them in kilns to achieve their final form and durability. Many workshops in Barlovento offer demonstrations and classes, allowing visitors to experience the process firsthand and even try their hand at creating their own pottery.

Decorative Pottery: A Fusion of Styles: In addition to traditional pottery, La Palma is also home to artists who experiment with contemporary styles and techniques, pushing the boundaries of this ancient craft. These modern potters draw inspiration from the island's landscapes, incorporating elements such as volcanic ash, sea shells, and plant fibers into their work, creating unique and innovative pieces that reflect both the heritage and the contemporary artistic spirit of La Palma.

Basketry

Basketry is another traditional craft that has been practiced on La Palma for centuries, utilizing the island's natural resources and showcasing the ingenuity of its people. The island's basket weavers, or "cesteros," use natural materials such as palm leaves, reeds, and straw to create a variety of products, from practical baskets for carrying goods to decorative items that adorn homes and add a touch of rustic charm.

> **El Paso: The Heart of Basketry:** El Paso is renowned for its basketry tradition, with many skilled cesteros continuing the techniques and patterns passed down through generations. The process of creating a basket involves several stages, including harvesting and preparing the natural materials, meticulously weaving them together to form the desired shape, and adding finishing touches to ensure both functionality and beauty. Each basket is a testament to the weaver's skill, patience, and creativity, with intricate patterns and sturdy construction that reflect the island's heritage.
>
> **Palm Leaf Hats: A Symbol of Tradition:** One of the most iconic products of La Palma's basketry tradition is the palm leaf hat, known as "sombrero de paja." These hats, woven from the leaves of the Canary Island date palm, are not only practical for protecting against the sun but also a symbol of the island's cultural identity. The process of making a palm leaf hat is labor-intensive, requiring careful selection and preparation of the leaves, followed by meticulous weaving to create the desired shape and pattern. The finished product is both functional

and beautiful, showcasing the skill and artistry of La Palma's cesteros.

Wood Carving

Wood carving is a cherished art form in La Palma, with skilled artisans transforming native woods into beautiful and functional objects that reflect the island's natural beauty and cultural heritage. The island's wood carvers, or "ebanistas," use traditional tools and techniques to create a range of products, from intricately carved furniture to decorative items that adorn homes and churches.

Santa Cruz de La Palma: Santa Cruz de La Palma, the island's capital, is a hub for wood carving, with workshops where ebanistas create a variety of pieces, from ornate furniture to religious icons. The wood used for these carvings is often sourced from local trees, such as pine, chestnut, and beech, adding to the authenticity and connection to the island's natural environment. The ebanistas take great pride in their work, with each piece reflecting their dedication to quality and craftsmanship.

Traditional Canarian Furniture: One of the most notable aspects of La Palma's wood carving tradition is the creation of traditional Canarian furniture. These pieces are characterized by their sturdy construction, intricate carvings, and practical design, reflecting the island's history and the ingenuity of its people. From intricately carved headboards and wardrobes to robust dining tables and chairs, Canarian furniture is both functional and decorative, adding a touch of elegance and tradition to any home.

Handcrafted Jewelry

Jewelry making is another vibrant aspect of La Palma's artistic tradition, with skilled artisans creating stunning pieces that combine traditional techniques with contemporary designs. The island's jewelers, or "orfebres," use a variety of materials, including precious metals, local stones, and shells, to create unique and beautiful jewelry that reflects the island's natural beauty and cultural heritage.

Tijarafe and Puntallana: Centers of Jewelry Making: The towns of Tijarafe and Puntallana are renowned for their jewelry workshops, where artisans craft a diverse range of pieces, from delicate earrings and bracelets to bold necklaces and rings. Many jewelers draw inspiration from the island's natural beauty, incorporating motifs such as flowers, waves, and stars into their designs, creating pieces that capture the essence of La Palma.

Traditional Filigree: One of the most distinctive styles of jewelry making in La Palma is filigree, a technique that involves twisting fine metal threads to create intricate and delicate patterns. This labor-intensive process requires a high level of skill and precision, resulting in stunning pieces that are both lightweight and visually captivating. Filigree jewelry is often used for special occasions, adding a touch of elegance and sophistication.

Festivals and Markets

La Palma's local art and craftsmanship are celebrated throughout the year at various festivals and markets, providing a platform for artisans to showcase their work and for visitors to experience the island's cultural heritage firsthand.

Fiesta de la Cruz: A Celebration of Creativity: The Fiesta de la Cruz, held in early May, is a vibrant festival that showcases the creativity and skill of La Palma's artisans. During this festival, towns and villages across the island are adorned with decorated crosses, many of which feature intricate floral arrangements, embroidery, and other handcrafted decorations. Each cross is a unique expression of the community's artistic talent and cultural identity.

Artisan Markets: A Shopper's Delight: Throughout the year, various towns on La Palma host artisan markets, where visitors can browse and purchase a wide range of handcrafted products. These markets offer everything from pottery and embroidery to jewelry and wood carvings, providing an opportunity to support local artisans and take home a piece of the island's artistic heritage.

Music and Dance Traditions
The Roots of La Palma's Music
The music of La Palma is a reflection of the island's history, which has been shaped by a confluence of cultures. The indigenous Benahoaritas, the original inhabitants of the island, laid the foundation for La Palma's musical traditions, with their ancient songs and dances reflecting their connection to the land and their unique cultural identity. The arrival of Spanish colonizers in the 15th century introduced new musical influences, including European instruments and musical styles. Over time, the island's music also absorbed elements from African and Latin American cultures, brought by immigrants and traders, further enriching its diversity.

Folías
One of the most iconic and beloved forms of traditional music in La Palma is the "folías." This genre, characterized by its

melancholic melodies and poetic lyrics, evokes a sense of longing and nostalgia, often expressing themes of love, loss, and the beauty of the island's natural landscapes. Folías are typically performed with the accompaniment of string instruments such as the timple, a small, five-stringed guitar unique to the Canary Islands, and the guitar, along with percussion instruments like the tambor (drum). The lyrics of folías often tell stories of the island's history, its people, and their daily lives, preserving cultural memories and traditions through song.

Malagueñas and Isas
Alongside folías, other traditional genres such as malagueñas and isas contribute to the richness of La Palma's musical heritage. Malagueñas are slow, expressive songs that often explore themes of longing, love, and the passage of time. Their melodies are often melancholic and introspective, inviting listeners to reflect on the emotions and experiences that shape human existence.

Isas, on the other hand, are more upbeat and lively, often performed at festivals, celebrations, and social gatherings. Their energetic rhythms and joyful melodies create a festive atmosphere and encourage participation and dance. Both malagueñas and isas showcase the islanders' deep connection to their land, their history, and their cultural identity, with music serving as a powerful vehicle for storytelling and cultural expression.

Traditional Instruments
The traditional music of La Palma is brought to life by a range of unique instruments, each with its own distinct voice and cultural significance.

> **The Timple:** The timple is perhaps the most emblematic instrument of La Palma and the Canary Islands as a whole. This small, five-stringed instrument, similar in appearance

to a ukulele, produces a bright and lively sound that is central to many traditional music genres. The timple's origins are thought to be linked to the arrival of Spanish settlers in the Canary Islands, and it has since evolved into a symbol of Canarian musical identity. Skilled timple players, known as timplistas, are revered for their ability to coax intricate melodies and rhythms from this humble instrument.

Laúd and Bandurria: Stringed Companions: The laúd, a type of lute, and the bandurria, a plucked string instrument similar to a mandolin, are also commonly used in traditional Canarian music. These instruments add depth and complexity to the music, with their rich harmonic textures and melodic capabilities. They are often played in tandem with guitars and timples, creating a vibrant and dynamic sound that is characteristic of Canarian folk music.

Percussion Instruments: The Rhythmic Backbone: Percussion instruments provide the rhythmic foundation for La Palma's traditional music, driving the melodies forward and adding energy and excitement to the performances. Traditional drums such as the tambor and caja (a type of snare drum) are commonly used, along with hand-held percussion instruments like castanets and maracas. These instruments add depth and texture to the music, creating a captivating auditory experience.

Dance Traditions

Dance is an integral part of La Palma's cultural expression, with traditional dances serving as a means of social interaction, community bonding, and celebration. These dances, often performed at festivals, religious events, and social gatherings, reflect the island's history, its people's joyous spirit, and their deep connection to their cultural roots.

The Baile del Vivo: A Living Tradition: The "baile del vivo" is one of the most popular and enduring traditional dances in La Palma. This lively dance is typically performed in pairs, with dancers moving in a series of intricate steps and patterns that mirror the rhythms of the accompanying music. The baile del vivo is often performed at festivals and celebrations, creating a vibrant and festive atmosphere that encourages participation and joy.

The Danza de las Libreas: The Danza de las Libreas is another iconic dance tradition in La Palma, particularly associated with the municipality of Tijarafe. This dance is performed during the annual Fiestas de Nuestra Señora de Candelaria, a religious festival that honors the island's patron saint. The dancers, dressed in elaborate costumes that often include masks and traditional attire, perform a series of choreographed movements to the accompaniment of live music. The Danza de las Libreas is a captivating spectacle that blends tradition, pageantry, and community celebration, showcasing the island's rich cultural heritage.

Carnival Dances: Carnival is a time of exuberant celebration in La Palma, and dance plays a central role in the festivities. During Carnival, the streets come alive with the sounds of drums, brass bands, and lively music, as dancers in colorful costumes and masks take to the streets, expressing their joy and creativity. The dances performed during Carnival are often energetic and improvisational, reflecting the festive spirit and the diverse cultural influences that have shaped the island's identity.

Modern Music and Dance

While traditional music and dance remain an essential part of La Palma's cultural identity, the island has also embraced modern influences, resulting in a dynamic and evolving artistic landscape. Contemporary musicians and dancers draw inspiration from both traditional and modern genres, creating a fusion of styles that reflects the island's ongoing cultural evolution.

Modern Folk Bands: Blending Old and New: Several modern folk bands on La Palma have gained popularity by blending traditional Canarian music with contemporary elements, such as electric instruments, modern production techniques, and diverse musical influences from around the world. These bands reinterpret traditional songs and compositions, infusing them with new energy and creating a fresh and innovative sound that appeals to both young and old audiences.

Contemporary Dance: La Palma's dance scene has also seen the rise of contemporary dance, with local choreographers and dancers exploring new forms of movement and expression. Contemporary dance performances often draw on a wide range of influences, from classical ballet to modern dance and performance art, pushing the boundaries of traditional dance forms and creating innovative and thought-provoking works.

Useful Tips
Money Matters

Currency and Exchange
La Palma, as part of Spain and the Canary Islands, uses the Euro (€) as its official currency. The Euro is divided into 100 cents, and common denominations include coins of 1, 2, 5, 10, 20, and 50 cents, as well as 1 and 2 Euro coins. Banknotes come in denominations of 5, 10, 20, 50, 100, 200, and 500 Euros.

Currency Exchange
While ATMs are widely available in towns and cities across La Palma, it's advisable to exchange some currency before arriving on the island, especially if you need cash immediately upon arrival. You can exchange currency at various locations, including banks, exchange offices, and sometimes at hotels and travel agencies. However, it's essential to be aware of commission fees and exchange rates, as these can vary between providers. Comparing rates and fees before exchanging your money can help you get the best deal.

Banking Services
La Palma offers a range of banking services to cater to both residents and visitors. Major banks such as Banco Santander, BBVA, and CaixaBank have branches on the island, providing a variety of services, including savings accounts, checking accounts, loans, and investment options. Online banking is also widely available, allowing customers to conveniently manage their finances from anywhere with an internet connection.

For visitors, it's important to carry a valid passport or other photo identification when using banking services, as this is often required for transactions such as currency exchange or cash withdrawals. Many banks in La Palma have extended hours during peak tourist seasons, making it easier for visitors to access their services and manage their finances while on the island.

Payment Methods
In La Palma, both cash and card payments are widely accepted. Major credit and debit cards, such as Visa, MasterCard, and American Express, are accepted in most shops, restaurants, and hotels. However, it's still a good idea to carry some cash for smaller establishments, local markets, and in case of emergencies. ATMs are readily available throughout the island, allowing you to withdraw cash as needed.

Cost of Living
The cost of living in La Palma can vary depending on your lifestyle and preferences. Generally, the island offers a range of options for accommodation, dining, and entertainment, catering to different budgets. Renting a property, whether it's a holiday home or a long-term rental, can be more affordable in La Palma compared to other parts of Spain, especially in the larger cities.

Groceries and everyday items are generally reasonably priced, and there are plenty of local markets where you can find fresh produce, local delicacies, and artisanal products at competitive prices. Dining out can range from budget-friendly local eateries to upscale restaurants, offering a variety of choices to suit your preferences and budget.

Taxes and Financial Regulations
Residents of La Palma are subject to Spanish tax laws, which include income tax, property tax, and value-added tax (VAT). The standard VAT rate in Spain is 21%, but reduced rates apply to certain goods and services, such as food and essential items. It's important for residents to stay informed about their tax obligations and seek professional advice from tax advisors or accountants if needed.

Economic Activities
La Palma's economy is diverse, with agriculture, tourism, and fishing being the main sectors. The island is renowned for its banana plantations, which are a significant source of income for many farmers and contribute to the island's agricultural exports.

Tourism plays a crucial role in La Palma's economy, with visitors attracted to the island's natural beauty, volcanic landscapes, hiking trails, stargazing opportunities, and cultural heritage. The tourism industry provides employment opportunities and supports a range of businesses, from hotels and restaurants to tour operators and souvenir shops.

The fishing industry also contributes to La Palma's economy, providing fresh seafood to local markets and restaurants. The island's fishermen utilize sustainable fishing practices to ensure the long-term health of the marine ecosystem.

Financial Planning and Savings
For residents of La Palma, financial planning and savings are important aspects of managing money effectively. Setting up a savings account, investing in a pension plan, and creating a budget can help ensure financial stability and long-term financial well-being. It's also beneficial to explore investment options, such as mutual funds, stocks, and real estate, to grow your wealth over time. Seeking advice from financial advisors can provide valuable insights and guidance tailored to your individual circumstances and financial goals.

Supporting Small Businesses
La Palma has a vibrant community of small businesses, including artisans, farmers, and entrepreneurs who contribute to the island's unique character and economic vitality. Supporting these businesses by shopping locally, choosing locally produced goods and services, and participating in community events can help

strengthen the local economy and preserve the island's cultural heritage.

Useful Contacts and emergency Information
Emergency Services
In any emergency situation, dialing 112 will connect you to the appropriate emergency services in La Palma. This universal emergency number in Spain provides access to the police, fire brigade, or ambulance services. It is a toll-free number available 24/7, and you can even call it without a SIM card in your phone. However, if you need to contact specific emergency services directly, the following numbers may be useful:

> **Civil Guard:** (+34) 922 412 385. The Civil Guard is a national law enforcement agency with a presence throughout Spain, including La Palma. They handle a wide range of responsibilities, including public safety, traffic control, and criminal investigations.

> **National Police:** (+34) 922 414 043. The National Police is another national law enforcement agency with jurisdiction in La Palma. They focus on urban areas and handle tasks such as crime prevention, public order, and traffic control.

Canary Police: (+34) 922 923 124. The Canary Police is a regional police force specific to the Canary Islands. They work in coordination with the National Police and the Civil Guard to ensure public safety and enforce local laws.

> **Fire Department:** (+34) 922 844 444. In case of fire or other emergencies requiring fire and rescue services, this number will connect you to the fire department in Las Palmas de Gran Canaria, which coordinates emergency response across the Canary Islands.

Medical Services

If you require medical assistance during your stay in La Palma, the following resources can provide the necessary care:

Hospital General de La Palma: (+34) 922 185 000. This is the main hospital on the island, offering a wide range of medical services, including emergency care, surgery, and specialized treatments.

Centro de Salud (Health Center): There are several health centers located throughout La Palma, providing primary healthcare services to residents and visitors. These centers offer general medical consultations, vaccinations, and basic treatments for common illnesses and injuries.

Pharmacies: Numerous pharmacies are available in towns and cities across La Palma, offering a wide range of over-the-counter medications, prescription medications (with a valid prescription), and other health and wellness products. Many pharmacies in tourist areas have extended hours to cater to the needs of visitors.

Transportation

La Palma offers various transportation options for getting around the island, including taxis, airport transfers, and public transportation.

Taxi Services
- Radio Taxi Santa Cruz de La Palma: (+34) 619 07 22 27
- Radio Taxi Los Llanos de Aridane: (+34) 922 40 35 40
- Radio Taxi Fuencaliente and Volcano Route: (+34) 639 35 79 89 / (+34) 618 42 02 41

Airport Transfers
- La Palma Airport BINTER: (+34) (922) or (928) 327 700
- CanaryFly: (+34) 928 018 500

Other Transportation:
- La Palma Airport: (+34) 91 321 1000
- Port of Santa Cruz de La Palma: (+34) 922 41 21 21

Tourist Information
The La Palma Tourism Office provides a wealth of information for visitors, including details on attractions, events, accommodations, and activities. They can assist with planning your itinerary, providing maps and brochures, and answering any questions you may have about the island.

> **La Palma Tourism Office:** Contact information may vary depending on the specific location, so it's best to check their official website or inquire at your accommodation for the nearest office.
>
> **La Palma Guided Walks:** If you're interested in exploring the island's natural beauty on foot, La Palma Guided Walks offers guided tours around the island, including the Roque de Los Muchachos area, home to the world-renowned observatory.

Other Useful Contacts
> **Local Police:** For non-emergency situations, you can contact the local police station in your area for assistance with matters such as noise complaints, lost property, or minor incidents.
>
> **Tourist Police:** The Tourist Police are specialized in assisting tourists with various issues, including lost

property, theft, and general inquiries. They can also provide information on local regulations and safety tips for visitors.

Embassies and Consulates: If you're a foreign visitor, it's advisable to have the contact information for your country's embassy or consulate in Spain. They can provide assistance in case of emergencies, such as lost passports or legal issues.

Emergency Contacts for Expats

thinkSPAIN: This online resource provides valuable information for expats living in Spain, including emergency phone numbers, alerts, and updates on local regulations and events.

7 Days Itinerary

Day 1: Arrival and Exploring the Historic Capital

Morning: Upon arrival at La Palma Airport, transfer to your chosen accommodation in Santa Cruz de La Palma, the island's charming capital. Settle into your hotel, guesthouse, or rental apartment, and take a moment to appreciate the relaxed atmosphere and the beauty of your surroundings.

Exploring the Old Town: Begin your La Palma adventure with a leisurely stroll through the historic center of Santa Cruz de La Palma. Wander through its cobblestone streets, lined with colorful colonial-style houses and adorned with intricate wooden balconies. Immerse yourself in the town's rich history as you visit Plaza España, the heart of the city, and the impressive Iglesia de El Salvador, a magnificent church with a blend of architectural styles.

Afternoon: Delve into La Palma's maritime history at the Naval Museum, housed in a unique building shaped like a replica of Christopher Columbus's ship, the Santa Maria. Explore the exhibits that showcase the island's role in the Age of Exploration, its shipbuilding traditions, and its connection to the sea.

Lunch with a View: Enjoy a traditional Canarian lunch at one of the local restaurants in Santa Cruz de La Palma. Savor local specialties such as "papas arrugadas" (wrinkled potatoes) with "mojo" sauce, a flavorful condiment made with local peppers, garlic, and herbs, and "vieja" (parrotfish), a delicious fish dish that reflects the island's coastal heritage.

Evening: As the day draws to a close, head to the Mirador de La Concepción, a viewpoint that offers breathtaking panoramic views of the island. Witness a stunning sunset over the Atlantic Ocean, casting a golden glow over the volcanic landscapes and the charming town below. Return to Santa Cruz for a relaxed dinner and a leisurely stroll along the Avenida Marítima, the seaside promenade that offers a vibrant atmosphere and stunning views of the harbor.

Day 2: Venturing North to Los Tilos and Los Sauces

Morning: Embark on a journey to the north of La Palma, starting with a visit to the lush Los Tilos Forest, one of the island's UNESCO Biosphere Reserves. Hike through the verdant trails, immersing yourself in the dense laurel forest, a relic of the ancient subtropical forests that once covered much of Europe. Marvel at the impressive waterfalls that cascade through the forest, creating a symphony of natural sounds. Don't miss the visitor center, where you can learn more about the unique flora and fauna that inhabit this protected ecosystem.

Afternoon: Continue your exploration of the north with a visit to the charming town of San Andrés y Sauces. Explore its historic center, with its traditional Canarian architecture, cobblestone streets, and picturesque plazas. Visit the Church of San Andrés, a beautiful example of the island's religious heritage, and the Plaza de Montserrat, a charming square surrounded by colorful houses and cafes.

Charco Azul: Spend the afternoon relaxing at Charco Azul, a series of natural seawater pools formed by volcanic rock. The crystal-clear water, sheltered from the waves of the Atlantic, provides a safe and refreshing environment for swimming and sunbathing. Enjoy the stunning coastal views and the tranquil atmosphere of this natural wonder.

Evening: Indulge in a delicious seafood dinner at one of the coastal restaurants in San Andrés y Sauces. Savor fresh fish dishes while enjoying the panoramic views of the Atlantic Ocean and the setting sun. After dinner, head back to your accommodation in Santa Cruz de La Palma for a restful night.

Day 3: Hiking in the Majestic Caldera de Taburiente National Park

Morning: Embark on an unforgettable adventure to the Caldera de Taburiente National Park, a geological wonder and a haven for nature lovers. Start your day at the Visitor Center in El Paso, the gateway to the park, where you can obtain maps, trail guides, and valuable information about the park's diverse ecosystems and hiking routes.

Hiking Through Volcanic Landscapes: Choose one of the park's well-marked trails based on your fitness level and interests. The trail to the Roque de Los Muchachos, the highest point on the island, offers breathtaking panoramic views of the caldera and the surrounding landscapes. Alternatively, hike into the heart of the caldera, descending through lush vegetation and alongside the Taburiente River, experiencing the park's unique geological formations and diverse flora and fauna.

Afternoon: Pack a picnic lunch and find a scenic spot within the caldera to enjoy your meal amidst the breathtaking scenery. The park is a paradise for nature enthusiasts, with dramatic landscapes, cascading waterfalls, and a variety of endemic plant and animal species. Spend the afternoon exploring more of the park's trails, discovering hidden corners and marveling at the natural beauty that surrounds you.

Evening: Return to El Paso and visit the Museum of the Silk Road, where you can learn about the island's fascinating silk-making tradition and its historical connections with the Silk Road. Enjoy dinner at a local restaurant in El Paso, savoring traditional Canarian specialties and the flavors of the island's cuisine. If the night is clear, consider driving to one of La Palma's renowned stargazing spots, such as Mirador del Llano del Jable, where you can marvel at the brilliance of the night sky and observe distant stars and galaxies.

Day 4: Discovering the West Coast - Tazacorte and Puerto Naos

Morning: Head to the west coast of La Palma and start your day in Tazacorte, a charming coastal town known for its sunny climate, historic architecture, and banana plantations. Explore the old quarter, with its narrow streets and colorful houses, and visit the Church of San Miguel, a beautiful example of Canarian religious architecture.

Banana Museum: Delve into the island's agricultural heritage with a visit to the Banana Museum in Tazacorte. Learn about the history and cultivation of bananas, one of La Palma's main agricultural products, and discover the importance of this industry to the island's economy and culture.

Afternoon: Enjoy a delicious seafood lunch at a beachfront restaurant in Tazacorte, savoring the fresh flavors of the island's coastal cuisine. Afterward, continue to Puerto Naos, a popular beach destination known for its black sand beach and lively atmosphere. Relax on the beach, take a refreshing dip in the Atlantic Ocean, or try some water sports, such as snorkeling or diving, to explore the underwater world.

Evening: Dine at a seaside restaurant in Puerto Naos, enjoying the relaxed atmosphere and the stunning views of the ocean as the sun sets. For a panoramic view of the sunset over the Caldera de Taburiente, head to the Mirador de La Cumbrecita, a viewpoint that offers breathtaking vistas of the island's volcanic landscapes.

Day 5: Southern Wonders - Fuencaliente and Volcanic Landscapes

Morning: Embark on a journey to the southern tip of La Palma and explore the unique landscapes of Fuencaliente. Start your day at the San Antonio Volcano Visitor Center, where you can learn about the island's volcanic history and geology through interactive exhibits and informative displays.

Volcanic Exploration: Hike around the San Antonio and Teneguía volcanoes, the youngest volcanoes on La Palma. The stark beauty of the volcanic landscapes, with their lava flows, craters, and unique rock formations, is truly awe-inspiring. Enjoy panoramic views of the Atlantic Ocean and the surrounding coastline, witnessing the power and beauty of nature's forces.

Afternoon: Visit the Salinas de Fuencaliente, a series of salt pans where sea salt is harvested using traditional methods. The contrast between the white salt crystals and the black volcanic soil creates a unique and photogenic landscape. Learn about the process of salt extraction and the importance of this industry to the island's economy and history. Enjoy a delicious lunch at a local restaurant near the salt pans, savoring dishes that feature locally harvested salt.

Evening: La Palma is renowned for its unique wines, produced from grapes grown in the island's volcanic soil. Visit a local winery in Fuencaliente for a tasting session, where you can sample the island's renowned Malvasia wines, known for their distinct flavors and aromas. Learn about the winemaking process, from grape cultivation to bottling, and appreciate the dedication and passion that goes into creating these exceptional wines. After your wine tasting experience, drive back to Santa Cruz de La Palma for the night.

Day 6: Exploring the East Coast - Puntallana and Los Sauces
Morning: Start your day in Puntallana, a charming village on the eastern coast of La Palma. Visit the Church of San Juan Bautista, a beautiful example of Canarian religious architecture, and the nearby Casa Luján, a traditional Canarian house that has been converted into a museum showcasing local crafts, customs, and traditions.

Los Sauces: Continue your journey to Los Sauces, another charming town on the east coast. Stroll through its historic center, admiring the traditional Canarian architecture and the colorful houses that line the streets. Visit the Church of Nuestra Señora de Montserrat, a beautiful church with a rich history, and the main square, a hub of local life and activity.

Afternoon: Spend the afternoon exploring the Los Tilos Forest, one of La Palma's natural treasures. Hike through its lush trails, enjoying the tranquility and the diverse plant life, including the ancient laurel trees that create a canopy overhead. The forest is a haven for birdwatchers, with a variety of species flitting among the trees.

Lunch in Los Sauces: Enjoy a delicious lunch at a local eatery in Los Sauces, savoring traditional Canarian dishes made from locally sourced ingredients. Experience the authentic flavors of the island's cuisine and the warm hospitality of its people.

Evening: Drive to Barlovento, a picturesque village known for its iconic dragon tree, a symbol of the Canary Islands. Explore the town's charming streets, admire the traditional architecture, and enjoy the serene atmosphere. Return to Santa Cruz de La Palma for the night, reflecting on your exploration of the island's eastern coast.

Day 7: Relaxation and Departure

Morning: Spend your last day in La Palma relaxing on one of the island's beautiful beaches. Whether you prefer the black sands of Puerto Naos, the secluded coves of Los Cancajos, or the natural pools of Charco Azul, take some time to unwind, soak up the sun, and enjoy the tranquility of the island's coastal beauty.

Lunch by the Sea: Enjoy a leisurely lunch at a beachfront restaurant, savoring the fresh seafood and local specialties one last time. Reflect on your La Palma adventure and the memories you've created while exploring the island's diverse landscapes and cultural heritage.

Afternoon: Explore the shops and markets of Santa Cruz de La Palma for souvenirs to take home as reminders of your trip. Look for local crafts, such as handmade pottery, embroidered textiles, and La Palma's famous cigars, each representing the island's unique traditions and craftsmanship. If time permits, visit one of the island's museums or cultural sites, such as the Insular Museum in Santa Cruz, to delve deeper into La Palma's history and culture.

Evening: Enjoy a farewell dinner at a local restaurant, savoring the flavors of Canarian cuisine and reminiscing about your week of adventures and discoveries on La Palma. As you transfer to La Palma Airport for your departure flight, carry with you the memories of an unforgettable journey through this enchanting island, its stunning landscapes, vibrant culture, and warm hospitality.

Estimated Budget for 7 Days

Planning a budget for a trip to La Palma, one of the Canary Islands, depends on several factors such as travel season, accommodation preferences, activities, and dining habits. Below is an estimated breakdown for a mid-range 7-day trip:

Flights
>**From Europe:** $100–$300 (round trip, budget airlines or connecting flights via Tenerife/Gran Canaria).
>**From the U.S.:** $600–$1,000+ (round trip, connecting flights).

Accommodation
>**Budget options (hostels, guesthouses):** $30–$60 per night.
>**Mid-range hotels or vacation rentals:** $80–$150 per night.
>**Luxury hotels/villas:** $200+ per night.
>
>**Estimated for 7 nights:**
>- Budget: $210–$420
>- Mid-range: $560–$1,050
>- Luxury: $1,400+

Transportation
>**Car rental:** $30–$50 per day, including insurance (~$250–$350 for 7 days). Public transport is limited.
>**Fuel:** ~$40–$70 for a week.
>**Taxis/transfers:** ~$10–$20 per trip for short distances.

Food and Drinks
>**Groceries:** $50–$80 for a week (if self-catering).
>**Dining out:**
>- Budget: $10–$15 per meal.

- Mid-range: $20–$35 per meal.
- High-end: $50+ per meal.

Estimated for 7 days:
- Budget: $150–$200
- Mid-range: $300–$500
- High-end: $700+

Activities

Hiking and nature trails: Mostly free or $5–$10 for permits (e.g., Los Tilos or Caldera de Taburiente).
Stargazing tours: $30–$60 per person.
Water activities (kayaking, snorkeling): $20–$50 per person.
Cultural experiences (museums, local tours): $10–$30 per ticket.
Estimated total for activities: $100–$250.

Miscellaneous

Travel insurance: $30–$50.
Souvenirs and shopping: $20–$100.

Estimated Total Budget (7 Days)

Budget traveler: $600–$900 per person.
Mid-range traveler: $1,200–$1,800 per person.
Luxury traveler: $2,500+ per person.

Prices can vary based on the season (high season is winter, especially December–March), so booking in advance can help save money. Let me know if you'd like help refining the budget!

Printed in Great Britain
by Amazon